Bureaucracy

Martin Albrow

University College, Cardiff

M
MACMILLAN

First published 1970 by Pall Mall Press Ltd
This edition published in 1970 by Macmillan & Co. Ltd
Reprinted 1978, 1979, 1982, 1984, 1985, 1989

Published by
MACMILLAN EDUCATION LTD
Houndmills, Basingstoke, Hampshire RG21 2XS
and London
Companies and representatives
throughout the world

Printed in Hong Kong

ISBN 0-333-11262-8

Contents

for my parents

Acknowledgements

The following read various drafts of this book and commented helpfully: Peter Calvert, University of Southampton; Professor S. E. Finer, University of Manchester; Anthony Giddens, King's College, Cambridge; Helmuth Heisler, University College, Cardiff; Michael Hill, University of Reading; Professor L. B. Schapiro, London School of Economics; Paul Wilkinson, University College, Cardiff. At the Pall Mall Press, Derick Mirfin provided invaluable support and prompting and laboured manfully with the text. The staff of the British Museum, the British Library of Political and Economic Science, and the Inter-Library Loan section of the library of University College, Cardiff have been unfailingly efficient. Sally Albrow has met all the importunate demands that an author makes of his wife, as well as looking after three children. I am very grateful to all these people, and absolve them of any responsibility for what follows.

Cardiff   Martin C. Albrow
October 1, 1969

Introduction

On January 29, 1968 the British House of Commons debated a Conservative motion condemning 'the continued growth of bureaucracy'. At the same time the motion deplored the failure of the Labour government to announce 'clear proposals to streamline the machinery of government and so to reduce the numbers employed in the public service'.[1] For most of the debate the two issues were treated as identical. But one member did express his disappointment that there was no discussion of more general ideas, and that 'bureaucracy' was being measured merely in numbers. He suggested that its essence was that 'the people who are appointed are not responsible to the people whose lives they affect'.[2] When a subsequent speaker tried to develop this argument he was told that it was not about the quality of government that they were debating but simply about the number of civil servants. He retorted that the 'words "continued growth of bureaucracy" imply a sneer'.[3] For him talk of bureaucracy raised more issues than the question of the size of the civil service.

It would be wrong to attribute these semantic difficulties to a decline in the capacity of British politicians to communicate with each other. In political debate, whether in the context of Stansted or Crichel Down, Medicare or the New Deal, and going back long before those controversies, 'bureaucracy' has been a term of strong emotive overtones and elusive connotations.

Those who turn to social and political science in the hope of finding illumination of this concept can only be disappointed. Political scientists, sociologists, management scientists have all devoted major pieces of theory and research to bureaucracy. The result of this academic division of labour has been a proliferation of concepts. In the search for terminological precision agreement on the concept has receded to the point where specialists in these neighbouring disciplines tolerate the existence of completely incompatible concepts of bureaucracy without comment. But, in spite of

13

prefacing their work with remarks such as: 'bureaucracy eludes definition';[4] or 'the term bureaucracy is devoid of any established meaning',[5] writers have gone on to discuss bureaucracy, whatever it may be. For social and political scientists are as much in agreement that 'the problems of bureaucracy' are important for academic thought and research, as politicians and the public are that they are worth debate.

The student coming to this field can be excused bewilderment. Sometimes 'bureaucracy' seems to mean administrative efficiency, at other times the opposite. It may appear as simple as a synonym for civil service, or it may be as complex as an idea summing up the specific features of modern organizational structure. It may refer to a body of officials, or to the routines of office administration.

This book is offered in aid of a clarification of this situation. It does not aim to set up a new theory of bureaucracy, nor even a new concept. (The reader will meet theories and concepts enough in the ensuing pages to make him welcome this act of self-abnegation on the part of the writer.) Nor is its aim to act as arbiter between the competing concepts, to label one or other as 'authoritative'. The task is conceived of as one of exposition: examining the wide variety of concepts of bureaucracy, investigating their relations, and explaining their development. In consequence 'bureaucracy' is always used in the text as reported speech, and never to refer to a concept of the writer's own.

It is hoped that this stock-taking will be useful at several levels. While the objective throughout has been to make the concept of bureaucracy intelligible to the newcomer to the subject, as so often happens with such exercises the author has been forced, in pursuing that purpose, to present new material. The modern concern for the logic of concept-formation has not been accompanied by an equal emphasis on the temporal and contextual limitations on the process of forming concepts in social science. The fact that the concept of bureaucracy has a history has been forgotten. The first chapter attempts to remedy this by showing how some of the most puzzling contradictions in modern concepts of bureaucracy arise in nineteenth-century theories. Partly as a consequence of this, the interpretation of Max Weber's concept of bureaucracy that is offered here differs markedly from recent accounts of this aspect of his work.

The same specialization which has involved the neglect of the origins of its concepts has given rise to genres of writing on bureaucracy quite isolated from each other. In consequence the modest objective of this book—to examine what is meant by those who write of bureaucracy—necessitates an immodest coverage of competing concepts in different disciplines. But the author believes that the novice has something to gain from this, and that the specialist who finds some part of the final chapters entirely familiar can still benefit from finding, juxtaposed to it, material from another specialty. In this last respect it is hoped that the bibliography will be a useful supplement to older and more general compilations by Merton and Eisenstadt.[6]

Although no attempt is made to produce a definitive concept of bureaucracy, the account in this book does seem to suggest some general conclusions on *desiderata* for any future conceptualizations in this field. The final chapter offers some suggestions for the alleviation of the present confusion on the basis of a brief consideration of some of the issues of concept-formation in social science that are raised in writing on bureaucracy. But such relief is more to be sought in a consciousness of the development and logical affiliations of the different concepts of bureaucracy. The author hopes that the remedy may be found in the analysis itself.

1970   MARTIN ALBROW

1/The Emergence of the Concept

The origin of the term

In a letter of July 1, 1764, the Baron de Grimm, the French philosopher, wrote: 'We are obsessed by the idea of regulation, and our Masters of Requests refuse to understand that there is an infinity of things in a great state with which a government should not concern itself. The late M. de Gournay[1] ... sometimes used to say: "We have an illness in France which bids fair to play havoc with us; this illness is called bureaumania". Sometimes he used to invent a fourth or fifth form of government under the heading of bureaucracy.'[2] A year later the same author wrote: 'The real spirit of the laws of France is that bureaucracy of which the late M. de Gournay ... used to complain so greatly; here the offices, clerks, secretaries, inspectors and *intendants* are not appointed to benefit the public interest, indeed the public interest appears to have been established so that offices might exist.'[3]

We are fortunate in having the invention of the word so precisely documented.[4] But it would be a mistake to confuse the coining of a term with the revelation of a new concept. Since de Gournay a very wide variety of ideas has been brought together under the heading of bureaucracy. Many have origins too remote to trace. Complaints about bad government must be as old as government itself. Concern that sovereigns should be served by diligent and faithful officials was a commonplace in political thought long before the eighteenth century. Machiavelli urged the prince to choose competent ministers, and to reward their fidelity so that they should not have to seek rewards from other sources.[5] Not even the idea of administrative efficiency is peculiar to modern, or indeed Western, thought. From 165 B.C. Chinese officials were selected by examination. Chinese administration was familiar with notions of seniority, merit ratings, official statistics and written reports and the writing of Shen Pu-hai (d. 337 B.C.) provided a set of principles which have been likened to twentieth-century theories of administration.[6]

Such ideas about government did not have to wait upon de

Gournay's flair for expression before they could be expressed. But there are two reasons why his formulation should be regarded as significant. He explicitly evokes the classical Greek classification of governments. In so doing he invents another type of government to add to long recognized forms, such as monarchy, aristocracy and democracy. He does not, therefore, conceive of eighteenth-century French government as some malformation of monarchy, such as tyranny. He is identifying a new group of rulers and a method of governing. The complaint against them is not that they are acting unlawfully, outside their proper authority, but that governing seems to have become an end in itself. This addition to the classical typology, albeit cursorily identified, must be regarded as an important conceptual innovation.

The second reason for emphasizing de Gournay's invention is related to the first, but is almost adventitious. It concerns the popularity the term has acquired. In the language of the eighteenth century 'bureau', as well as signifying a writing-table, already meant a place where officials worked. The addition of a suffix, derived from the Greek word for 'rule', resulted in a term with considerable power to penetrate other cultures. The Greek concepts of government had long been domesticated in the major European languages. The new term could easily undergo the same transliterations as 'democracy' or 'aristocracy'. It rapidly became part of an international vocabulary of politics. The French *bureaucratie* rapidly became the German *Bureaukratie* (later *Bürokratie*), the Italian *burocrazia*, and the English 'bureaucracy'. Furthermore, on analogy with the derivatives of democracy, with bureaucracy went bureaucrat, bureaucratic, bureaucratism, bureaucratist and bureaucratization.

It is, therefore, not surprising that early dictionary definitions of bureaucracy are highly consistent, both with each other and with de Gournay. The Dictionary of the French Academy accepted the word in its 1798 supplement and defined it as: 'Power, influence of the heads and staff of governmental bureaux.'[7] An 1813 edition of a German dictionary of foreign expressions defined bureaucracy as: 'The authority or power which various government departments and their branches arrogate to themselves over fellow citizens.'[8] An Italian technical dictionary of 1828 referred to it thus: 'Neologism, signifying the power of officials in public administration.'[9] The French Academy also accepted 'bureaucratic' in reference to 'the influence of governmental bureaux, and also a regime where bureaux multiply without need'. This dual meaning attributed to 'bureaucratic' gives the first hint of the complex development the concept was to undergo.

Early nineteenth-century concepts

In spite of its origins in the thinking of the French physiocrats and its acceptance by the lexicographers, the early use of the term 'bureaucracy' seems to have been confined to the works of polemicists and novelists. Balzac was largely responsible for popularizing the word in French. His novel of 1836, *Les Employés*, was actually half treatise on the ways of bureaucracy. His vituperative tone is a good example of a way of thinking that has never ceased to have its adherents:

> Since 1789 the State, or if you like to have it so, *La Patrie*, has taken the place of the sovereign. The clerks no longer take their instructions directly from one of the first magistrates in the realm . . . and thus Bureaucracy, the giant power wielded by pigmies, came into the world. Possibly Napoleon retarded its influence for a time, for all things and all men were forced to bend to his will. . . . Bureaucracy was definitely organized, however, under a constitutional government with a natural kindness for mediocrity, a predilection for categorical statements and reports, a government as fussy and meddlesome, in short, as a small shopkeeper's wife.[10]

So successful was Balzac in projecting his image of bureaucracy that when Le Play attempted the first serious French consideration of the concept in 1864, he felt obliged to apologize for 'this hybrid word created by a light literature'.[11] The 1873 edition of Littré's dictionary still felt that the word was a barely correct neologism.[12] Even in 1896 a French political dictionary expressed the view that the word originated in Germany and was only popularized in France by Balzac.[13]

The idea that the term came from Germany was not surprising. During the French Revolution German newspapers reported events in France and spoke of bureaucracy without further explanation.[14] Outside the press the earliest known German reference to bureaucracy would appear to be by Christian Kraus, one of Kant's colleagues. In a letter of 1799 he contrasted Prussia with England, where, he argued, the populace remained the rock-fast base of the pyramid of state, while 'the Prussian state, far from being an un-limited monarchy . . . is but a thinly veiled aristocracy, . . . which blatantly rules the country as a bureaucracy'.[15] The term, however, did not immediately enter serious political writing. Wilhelm von Humboldt's essay of 1792, *An Attempt to Determine the Limits of the Effectiveness of the State*, failed to mention bureaucracy. But its theme, the fear that an increase of state authority entailed the growth of administration, and the fear that the affairs of state were becoming mechanical while men were being transformed into machines, was later to become commonplace in polemics against bureaucracy.[16]

Humboldt's fears were echoed in a letter of the Freiherr vom Stein in 1821. Stein did not shrink from indicting the system he had administered and reformed after the Prussian defeat by Napoleon in 1806. But he spoke of *Büralisten* rather than bureaucrats:

> We are ruled by buralists—salaried, with a knowledge of books, with no cause to support, and without property. . . . In these four points is summed up the spirit of our own and similar lifeless governmental machines: salaried, hence striving to maintain and increase the number of those with salaries; with a knowledge of books, hence not living in the real world, but in one of letters; with no cause to support, for they are allied with none of the classes of citizens that constitute the state, they are a caste in their own right, the caste of clerks, without property, and therefore unaffected by its fluctuations. Come rain or sunshine, whether taxes rise or fall, whether long-established rights are destroyed or preserved, it makes no difference to them. They draw their salaries from the exchequer and write, write, write, in silence, in offices behind closed doors, unknown, unnoticed, unpraised, and they bring up their children to be equally usable writing machines.[17]

This passage was used by Karl Heinzen, a radical who had to flee from Prussia. He included it in his polemic of 1845 against Prussian bureaucracy, but he substituted 'bureaucrat' for 'buralist' (as well as adding embellishments of his own).[18]

Probably the work of Johan Görres did most to publicize the concept of bureaucracy in early nineteenth-century Germany. Publicist, romantic, founder of the newspaper the *Rheinische Merkur*, he became so important an opponent of the monarchy that he also was forced to leave Prussia. Using the classical typology of government to provide the elements of his analysis he developed a theory of the basis of national unity. Monarchical and democratic elements had to be combined to provide co-operation and mutual respect between rulers and ruled. Bureaucracy was the result when these conditions were not fulfilled. In *Europe and the Revolution* (1821), he saw bureaucracy as the civil institution analogous to the standing army. It was based on the same principles of discipline, promotion, group honour and centralization. The administrative techniques which filled the gap left by the lack of trust between rulers and ruled became principles of state. Bureaucracy succeeded 'in extending the principle of subordination, which was basic to its own development, from its own organism to the subject population, to conglomerate them gradually into masses, in which people only counted as numbers, deriving value not from their selves, but from their positions'.[19]

It is important to note a dual emphasis in these early ideas of bureaucracy. It is viewed not only as a form of government where power is in the hands of officials; it is also a collective designation for those officials. If one considers the concepts of aristocracy and democracy it is possible to see how this could have happened. 'Aristocracy' is used almost exclusively to refer to a particular social stratum, rather than to a form of government. On the other hand 'democracy' is normally taken to refer to the institutional forms through which the will of a population may be realized. (This is a long way, incidentally, from the Aristotelian concept of democracy as the rule of a class.) Either emphasis was possible in the early conceptualizations of bureaucracy. The early writers on the subject perceived clearly that this new form of government was related to a new element in the system of social stratification. It did not seem inappropriate, given the use of the term 'aristocracy', to refer to that new element as 'the bureaucracy'.

In English syntax the presence or absence of an article normally signifies which of the two aspects of the concept is being stressed: 'the' or 'a bureaucracy' referring to a body of bureaucrats; 'bureaucracy' designating procedures of administration. In more recent jargon, the concept of bureaucracy has comprised both institutional and associational aspects. On this simple, but vital, distinction depend two basic modes of sociological thinking: the analysis of action, and the analysis of groups. If this distinction had always been recognized much of the confusion in the literature on bureaucracy could have been avoided.

The English theory

It is largely through translations from the German literature that we are able to determine the time of the reception of 'bureaucracy' into English. An earlier work by Görres, *Germany and the Revolution* (1819), was translated into English in two separate versions in 1820.[20] In both cases direct translation of *bureaukratisch* into 'bureaucratic' was avoided.[21] On the other hand an 1832 translation of the travel letters of a German prince reported his view thus: 'The Bureaucracy has taken the place of the Aristocracy, and will perhaps soon become equally hereditary.'[22] The 1827 edition of Johnson's *Dictionary* had no entry for the word. On the other hand *The Popular Encyclopaedia* of 1837 (itself based on the great German *Conversationslexicon*), contained an item on the 'bureau system, or bureaucracy'.[23]

These translations encouraged a contrast to be drawn between England and the Continent which became a standard part of nineteenth-century observations on bureaucracy. In the great periodicals, such as *Blackwood's* or the *Westminster Review*, commentary on continental institutions almost invariably included a self-congratulatory rider on how different things were in England. Carlyle's terse comment in 1850 on bureaucracy—'the continental nuisance . . . I can see no risk or possibility in England. Democracy is hot enough here . . .'—summed up the prevailing English judgement on the subject.[24] Even Herbert Spencer, who was so concerned to establish the limits and functions of the state, was content to mention bureaucracy in the context of comments on France.[25] However it should not be thought that the assessments of bureaucracy in the nineteenth-century journals were invariably as perfunctory as Carlyle's. Many of them anticipated points upon which whole theories have been centred. An essay of 1836 on the French educational system observed that, for any defect in bureaucratic machinery, the remedy always took the form of further machinery.[26] In 1842 J. S. Blackie, a commentator on the German scene, considered that the way in which the Prussian bureaucracy monopolized the intelligence of the nation was detrimental to energy and enterprise outside it, and resulted in submissiveness and servility.[27]

This last point was one which particularly impressed the major English writer on bureaucracy in the nineteenth century, John Stuart Mill. In his *Principles of Political Economy* (1848), he set himself against 'concentrating in a dominant bureaucracy all the skill and experience in the management of large interests, and all the power of organized action, existing in the community'. He saw it as 'a main cause of the inferior capacity for political life which has hitherto characterized the over-governed countries of the continent'.[28]

In *On Liberty* (1859), Mill developed these views still further. The dangers of bureaucracy were singled out for the peroration of that immensely influential essay. He held them to constitute the third and most important reason for objecting to government interference, even when it did not infringe liberty. For, the more functions a government took on the more careers it offered, and thus the more hangers-on it attracted. The more efficient the machinery of administration, the more it would monopolize the talent of the nation. To be admitted to the bureaucracy would be the summit of ambition, while outside it there would be few qualified to criticize. Both governors and governed become the slaves of the bureaucracy, and no reform would be possible. 'Where everything is done through the bureaucracy, nothing to which the bureaucracy is really adverse can be done at all.'[29]

The concept of bureaucracy reached its full importance in Mill's political theory in his *Considerations on Representative Government* (1861). In comparing types of government, he argued that the only form, other than the representative, which had high political skill and ability was bureaucracy, even when it went under the name of a monarchy or aristocracy. 'The work of government has been in the hands of governors by profession; which is the essence and meaning of bureaucracy.'[30] Such a government 'accumulates experience, acquires well-tried and well-considered traditional maxims, and makes provision for appropriate practical knowledge in those who have the actual conduct of affairs'.[31] But, on the debit side, bureaucracies die of routine. 'They perish by the immutability of their maxims.'[32] Only the popular element in government was capable of allowing the conceptions of a man of original genius to prevail over trained mediocrity. The governments of China and Russia were examples of what happened when the bureaucracy held power. Skilled administration was certainly necessary, but it had to be under the general control of bodies representative of the whole people.[33]

Mill's formulations were brief but influential. The sharp antinomy he discerned between bureaucracy and democracy has been examined repeatedly since his writing. But just as important as the substantive issue of the relations of the administrative system to constitutional democracy—which his concept of bureaucracy highlighted—was the analytical issue of what criteria were appropriate for classifying governments. Mill's emphasis, in contrasting democracy and bureaucracy, was on the locus of decision-making and real power, not upon the formal processes of selection for supposedly sovereign bodies. This was of great importance in shaping Mosca's ideas (see chapter 2), and, more immediately, proved a very suitable theme for more concrete elaboration by the most incisive nineteenth-century commentator on the English constitution, Walter Bagehot.

In *The English Constitution* (1867), Bagehot warned against any undue admiration for the Prussian state system that might be occasioned by its recent military successes. The successes of bureaucracy could only be limited. It depended on routine which, adapted to one situation, was insufficiently flexible to meet new problems. Only sixty years before the Prussian system was held to be 'dead and formal'. In fact Bagehot was less impressed than Mill with the efficiency of bureaucracy. 'The truth is that a skilled bureaucracy—a bureaucracy trained from early life to its special avocation—is, though it boasts the appearance of science, quite inconsistent with the true principles of the art of business.'[34] This is not to say that Bagehot was against expertise, of the proper kind and in the right place. He did not approve of the American system of wholesale administrative changes when a new party came to power. (He was writing before the reforms made by President Cleveland.) He indicted the classes from whose ranks English administrators were drawn for ignorance and lack of business education. He found the arrangement of public offices in England to be casual and unsystematic.

But, in spite of these defects, for Bagehot the great virtue of English administration was that a frequent change of ministers never allowed it to sink into routine. New men, sensitive to outside opinion, were always available to re-invigorate the administrative process. Bagehot was contrasting bureaucracy, unchecked by wider experience and opinion, with public administration in a system of parliamentary government. But he did not make use of Mill's abstract justification that efficiency had to be tempered in the interests of liberty. Public administration in a democracy was actually more efficient. He likened it to the success of the great joint-stock banks, the success of which depended 'on a due mixture of special and non-special minds—of minds which attend to the means, and of minds which attend to the end'.[35] This contrast between business efficiency and bureaucracy was to become a standard one in the work of twentieth-century conservative ideologists (see chapter 4).

It would be wrong to suppose that the high opinion Englishmen had of their own administrative system was simply a reflection of insularity or jingoism. It was a view shared by very many continental scholars. From the standpoint of a political science (*Staatswissenschaft*) based in universities, German writers attempted to describe the contrast between continental bureaucracy and English administration in precise terms. Eduard Fischel's *Die Verfassung Englands* (1862) attempted to draw a lesson for German statesmen from the English experience of self-government. In German doctrine the unity of the state could not be secured without centralization. The high degree of autonomy enjoyed by the English gentry in local government was unthinkable. But, argued Fischel, it was a mistake to think that centralization and self-government were incompatible. Without the hierarchy and authoritarianism that characterized Germany, English local government observed both the common law and the wishes of parliament. The real incompatibility was between bureaucracy and self-government.[36]

Both the greater climate of freedom in England and the greater sophistication of continental political analysis would appear to be confirmed by the fact that what is probably the first empirical study of bureaucracy was written by an Austrian for the *Contemporary Review* in 1880. Friedrich von Schulte's "Bureaucracy and its Operation in Germany and Austria-Hungary" repeated Fischel's argument that the Germans regarded self-government as a direct weakening of both crown and bureaucracy. In Germany there was 'a many-sided antithesis between the bureaucratic class and citizen class'.[37] But 'the tumour of bureaucracy',[38] had taken too deep a hold. 'Everybody blames the Bureaucracy and asks from it every-thing he needs.'[39] Much in Schulte's analysis anticipates the problem-settings of modern sociology. He set himself the task of reviewing 'the organization of the hierarchy of officials in its grada-tion, titles, etc.; their pecuniary position; the cost of the public administration; the admission of non-officials into the hierarchical order and society; the relation of the bureaucracy to self-govern-ment'.[40] In addition he compared the proportion of officials to general population in each of the major German states.

Towards the end of the century the self-confidence of English writers on bureaucracy began to diminish. The reforms of the civil service, notably those of 1870, took it nearer to, rather than further from, the continental services. In a speech in 1884 Sir Stafford Northcote, who had himself played an important part in the incep-tion of these reforms, spoke of the dangers of a bureaucratic despotism in which 'the permanent officials will take the manage-ment of affairs into their hands, and Parliament will have little to do'.[41] No longer could bureaucracy be regarded as a foreign form of government. The danger was nearer home, and attacks on it became increasingly strident.

In the same year as Northcote's speech Herbert Spencer pub-lished a vehement attack on state intervention. In four essays in the *Contemporary Review* he castigated the Liberals for espousing state intervention and departing from their earlier concern for free-dom of contract.[42] He detected a development analogous to that experienced under continental bureaucracies. 'Increasing power of a growing administrative organization is accompanied by decreas-ing power of the rest of society to resist its further growth and control. The multiplicity of careers opened by a developing bur-eaucracy tempts members of the classes regulated by it to favour its extension, as adding to the chances of safe and respectable places for their relatives.'[43]

Also in 1884, F. C. Montague's *The Limits of Individual Liberty* developed the same theme. On the Continent men had to acquiesce in a regulated servitude. But there was no need to regard this as inevitable in England. An employed bureaucracy regularly became a governing bureaucracy, inflexible, fond of power, but enslaved by routine. By accustoming men to heavy taxation and paternal care it 'stimulates all tendencies to communism'.[44] But in England, Parliament, the courts and municipal liberties ensured that administration and the community were identified, and bureaucracy prevented. By the turn of the century it was recognized that bureaucracy had already arrived. One writer even argued that agitation for female suffrage was simply an irrelevance, diverting attention from the real problem of bureaucratic government.[45] But, as late as 1914, it was still possible to insist that the phenomenon, like the word, was an intrusion from abroad and not yet deeply rooted in British government.[46]

The English nineteenth-century theory of bureaucracy was most lucidly summarized in the historian Ramsay Muir's essay of 1910, "Bureaucracy in England". For him bureaucracy meant 'the exercise of power by professionalized administrators'.[47] 'The most steady, persistent and powerful influences in the government of England are those of the great permanent officials.'[48] But the idea that it was 'essentially un-English' and a growth of the last few years, he criticized strongly. For more than seventy years it had been growing steadily. There had been 'the most astonishing conspiracy of silence to maintain this illusion' that the English system was non-bureaucratic.[49]

Muir's dismissal of the English belief in their freedom from bureaucracy was an early expression of twentieth-century pessimism on this subject. Certainly this belief, illusion or not, and the English writing on this theme, of which it was a part, have largely been forgotten. But its image of a society not governed by officials was a major influence on the much more developed and profound continental writing, which will be discussed in the remainder of this chapter and the next.

Continental theory

The contrast between English and German writing on bureaucracy was immense. The English writers feeling safely distant from the continental type of government, did not have to concern themselves with the technical minutiae of its operation. In their broad comparative perspective all European countries were of the same type: places where officials ruled. In any classification of governments bureaucracy had to appear as a major, and fortunately foreign, variety. The English system of administration did not demand technical text books on, or degrees in, a science of the state, and criticism of this system did not have direct repercussions on the personal liberty of the writer. The highly centralized German states were governed by professional officials, working on the basis of official doctrines on administration. Hence writing on the theme of bureaucracy was either technical and an adjunct to legal science, or it was an opposition literature, regarded by the state as subversive. Lorenz von Stein, author of the great treatise on German administrative theory, tried, with unconscious humour, to put the best possible complexion on this contrast. 'It is true that the French and the English, whom we always regard as models, have neither the concept nor the system of the State. But it is also true that they have absolutely no science of the State. This is precisely what puts the German genius so high above that of other nations, that we are striving to possess such a science.'[50]

It is vital for the understanding of the work of Max Weber (discussed in the next chapter), that the contrasting *contexts* of German and English writing on bureaucracy are recognized. In Germany the idea of bureaucracy was intimately connected with radical changes in both the theory and practice of administration following the Prussian defeat by Napoleon in 1806. It would be too long a task to pursue German administrative theory back into the eighteenth century and further.[51] But, to characterize it briefly, it was dominated by the concept of the *collegium*, a body of officials charged with advising the ruler and taking responsibility for a particular function of government, such as finance or law and order. This responsibility was a collective one, and there was considerable scope within the *collegium* for the clash of ideas and interests. After 1806 the collegial system was replaced by what was called the *Bureau-* or *Einheitssystem*, in which responsibility was clearly vested in an individual at each level of authority up to a minister.

The difference between the two systems was examined at length in treatises on administration.[52] The collegial form had the advantages of subjecting decisions to discussion from many points of view. It developed norms which limited arbitrariness, and ensured that business was strictly supervized. But decisions only emerged slowly, trivialities absorbed an inordinate amount of time, and responsibility could never be clearly pinned to an individual. The bureau system secured individual responsibility, and hence decisiveness, unity and energy. It was able to draft documents speedily, and saved on personnel expenses. But it did have the danger of delivering administration up to the idiosyncrasies of the individual official.

Now it became a matter of considerable argument whether the bureau system and bureaucracy were to be identified with each other. As we have seen the idea of bureaucracy as rule by officials was already current in Germany. Since the new system of administration was widely recognized as increasing the power of officials the identification of it with bureaucracy was not a difficult step to take. This can be clearly illustrated from the great *Brockhaus* encyclopaedia of 1819:

> The modern form of public administration executes with the pen everything which previously would have been done by word of mouth. Hence many pens are set into motion. In every branch of administration bureaux or offices have multiplied, and have been accorded so great a power over citizens that in many countries a veritable bureaucracy, rule by offices, has developed. This bureaucracy becomes increasingly dangerous as the previous custom of conducting business through *collegia* falls into disuse. The directors of a bureau, in addition to their authority over its personnel, have acquired an often inordinate amount of power over citizens at large.[53]

For opponents of the German state the identification of the bureau system and bureaucracy made an extremely useful polemical point. Thus the socialist Karl Heinzen offered an apparently neutral and technical definition of bureaucracy as 'an administrative structure where a single official controls the administration, as opposed to the collegial structure where several officials work under a head, but with definite rights to participate in administration on a collective basis'.[54] But Heinzen then went on to make use of all the negative connotations of bureaucracy as government by officials. In its spirit it combined arrogance with servility; intended as an instrument it acquired for itself the characteristics of unlimited power. Prussian officialdom was particularly sensitive to this kind of criticism (Heinzen was forced to leave Germany) because it did not necessarily have to come from socialist quarters. It was quite consistent with this idea of bureaucracy to call on the monarch to re-establish true statesmanship, as another critic of bureaucracy, Friedrich Rohmer, did when he argued that the only tangible result of the 1848 revolutions was to put new men into the old administrative system.[55]

By and large the 'official' representatives (and it must be remembered that professors were employees of the state) of German political science tried to maintain the distinction between the new system of administration and bureaucracy. Sometimes this distinction simply took the form of asserting that the term 'bureaucracy' was used in two quite different ways, which were not to be confused with each other.[56] Sometimes, as in the eleventh edition of *Brockhaus*, the term was reserved for the case where officials controlled state affairs, and the new administrative structure was simply designated *Bureausystem*.[57] Lorenz von Stein preferred the latter usage.[58]

This semantic confusion, coupled with the prevalence of polemics against bureaucracy, prompted the first academic analysis of the concept of bureaucracy in 1846.[59] Robert von Mohl, professor of political science at Heidelberg, suggested that historically the meaning of bureaucracy as the 'bureau system' had priority, and had only recently been supplanted by the popular abusive meaning. But as a term of abuse von Mohl found that bureaucracy had a variety of connotations, depending on which social group was uttering the complaint. The privileged classes complained of loss of privileges, the commercial classes of interference in commerce, artisans of paperwork, scientists of ignorance, statesmen of delay. Behind all these expressions of complaint lay a common idea of bureaucracy as 'the false conception of the tasks of the state, implemented by a numerous . . . body of professional officials'.[60]

Von Mohl was a standard authority to be quoted in nineteenth-century encyclopaedias. Hence it is important to note a shift of emphasis in his concept of bureaucracy. Earlier concepts were part of a system of concepts, however rudimentary. De Gournay thought of bureaucracy as one of four types of government, Heinzen as one of two types of administrative system. Von Mohl simply relied upon finding a common meaning in colloquial usage. Where citizens complained about the state, there, *ipso facto*, was bureaucracy. Such complaints could be assuaged by governmental attention to improving education, reducing form-filling and by general goodwill. Compared with a writer such as Mill, von Mohl was simply considering contingent features of bureaucracy, superficial symptoms rather than the underlying condition. (These were frequently referred to as bureaucratism.) Since any form of government was likely to engender similar complaints it was an easy step to regard any system of administration, good or bad, as bureaucracy, and this somewhat vapid usage, very popular in the twentieth century, emerged soon after von Mohl's essay.[61]

Bureaucratism—the behaviour and attitudes of professional officials which offended the citizen—received its fullest discussion in the work of Josef Olszewski, a Polish lawyer, in 1904.[62] His long account of administrative abuses owed much to von Mohl. This was also the theme of the first serious French account of bureaucracy by the great social scientist, Frederic Le Play.[63] Indeed, more explicitly than any other writer, Le Play located bureaucracy in the middle ranks of officialdom. For him it meant the dissemination of authority among minor officials, absorbed in details, intent upon complicating business, and suppressing initiative in others.

The popular success of Balzac's characterization of bureaucracy had seemed to remove the topic from serious political analysis in France.[64] The classic analysis of the French governmental system by de Tocqueville made only passing reference to bureaucracy and concentrated on the processes of centralization.[65] This factor, together with the absence of the bureaucratic-collegial dichotomy of German administrative science accounted for the distinctiveness of Le Play's approach. Sharply distinguishing bureaucracy from centralization, he attempted to provide a structural and motivational explanation of the behaviour of middle-ranking officials.

Le Play's concern was with organizational structure rather than with legal concepts. This concern with the quality rather than the legality of administration had something in common with Bagehot's concern for business efficiency. It clearly opened the way for comparisons between governmental and private methods of administration. When Pierre Leroy-Beaulieu, a liberal professor of politics, wrote on the modern state and its functions in 1890 he took it for granted that one could talk of bureaucracy in joint-stock companies.[66] He found this form of bureaucracy far more supple and better staffed than the bureaucracy of the state. Such comparisons were precursors of the twentieth-century concern with developing a general theory of organization.

The major nineteenth-century themes

It is possible to distinguish three major concepts in nineteenth-century writing on bureaucracy. Writers such as de

Gournay or Mill saw bureaucracy as a major form of government, to be compared and contrasted with monarchy, democracy or aristocracy. German administrative theorists and polemicists, such as Heinzen, concentrated on the particular form nineteenth-century German administrative arrangements took. Von Mohl, Olszewski, or Le Play took their cue from popular discontent with government and saw the essence of bureaucracy in the officiousness of the paid civil servant.

In spite of the twentieth-century neglect of this literature it is clearly not insignificant, either in quantity or quality. The three major concepts distinguished here will have an important place in the subsequent account of twentieth-century writing. Indeed it is only by referring to the substance of this chapter that it is possible to make sense of later conceptual paradoxes. Two incompatible concepts—bureaucracy as administrative efficiency and bureaucracy as administrative inefficiency—compete for space in twentieth-century theory. This is not an incomprehensible vagary of modern social science, but a development of nineteenth-century argument, mediated by the giant contributions of Mosca, Michels and Max Weber.

But if it is the case that the nineteenth-century writing is important, both in its own right and for the understanding of later developments, we are forced to ask why it has been lost to view. Mosca, Michels and Max Weber appear both to have transformed the theory of bureaucracy and to have concealed its origins. A brief and tentative answer to this puzzle may be offered if we consider how writing on bureaucracy differed from the work of the major political ideologists of the nineteenth century.

With the exception of Mill, none of the writers considered hitherto comes into the category of influential system builders. In the great ideological systems one may distinguish two major theories of the distribution of power in society. In the one, those who held power were justified in either religious or secular metaphysical terms. They had a mission to perform for God or society and their servants, the public officials, shared in that purpose. In the other, power was the product of a group's place in the economic order of society. Officials were simply the agents of government, the instruments of the dominant class. We can see these two essentially simple standpoints elaborated by Hegel and Marx respectively. For neither did bureaucracy pose a problem of analysis since it could not be conceived of as a separate element distinct from the state or the economic order. (Marx's position will be examined in detail in chapter 4.)

But for lesser figures, more concerned to confront the system with the facts, bureaucracy posed a severe analytical problem. Each of the three major concepts of bureaucracy that have been distinguished here is focused on the paradoxical position of the permanent, paid government official. For those who had faith in a monarch or a sovereign people the official appeared more and more distinct from the source of his authority, often in opposition to it, and certainly devoid of any charisma. For those who saw government as simply an aspect of the activity of men pursuing their economic interests, the position of the official was paradoxical: his involvement in power did not stem from his position in society; on the contrary, his position in society was derived from his place in government.

The facts were noted. But they were not accommodated in any major theoretical system. Indeed when writers on bureaucracy considered, as they all did, how it might be combated, their resort was to the traditional formulas. Sometimes they called upon the monarch to re-establish his authority. More frequently the remedy was sought in the devolution of power into the hands of traditional interest groups: aristocracies, landowners, businessmen or tax-paying citizens. What was not accepted was that the power of the permanent paid official was an inevitable feature of modern government. Therefore the great systems were not refurbished to find a place for bureaucracy. It was only with Mosca, Michels and Max Weber that the systematic conceptualizations of the importance of the permanent paid official became more adequate to the place he already held in society.

2/The Classical Formulations

Mosca and Michels

In some rather obvious ways Gaetano Mosca's work belongs to the nineteenth century. His classic work, *Elementi di Scienza Politica* (translated as *The Ruling Class*) appeared in 1895.[1] His starting point was a criticism of the traditional classification of governments. Broad comparative scope and the widest possible use of historical evidence were characteristic of the works of Comte and Spencer, the two writers Mosca found it most important to analyse. Moreover, he was well aware of the nineteenth-century tradition of writing on bureaucracy. Mill and Fischel were two of the writers he listed as having most influence upon his own theories.[2]

The ingredients of Mosca's work were not new. But his combination of them was novel, and provides the justification for discussing him outside the nineteenth-century context. At last the concept of bureaucracy and dissatisfaction with the traditional scheme of governmental types were incorporated into a major comparative analysis of politics. Against a classification of governments which had endured for over two thousand years Mosca clearly felt it was not too much to pit the major part of his fifty years of intellectual product. In 1884, in the first chapter of his first book, he wrote: 'Now when we come to the classification of governments which goes back to Aristotle and is still in our day universally accepted: into democratic, aristocratic, or monarchic types . . . then we should expect that classification also to be based on the most important, the essential characteristics of government and not on mere trivialities and appearances.'[3] In 1933, in the last chapter of his last book, he argued that this classification had two defects. It was 'based on observation of a single moment in the evolution of political organisms', and it took into account their 'formal rather than the really substantial differences'.[4]

In the terminology of traditional logic Mosca was seeking a new *fundamentum divisionis*, a principle of classification, which would get behind the language of authority and illuminate the reality of political processes.[5] He saw the core of this reality in the facts of power. In the following general proposition he summed up these facts: 'In all regularly constituted societies in which something called a government exists, . . . the ruling class, or rather, those who hold the exercise of the public power, will always be in a minority and below them we find a numerous class of persons who never do, in any real sense, participate in government but merely submit to it: and these may be called the ruled class.'[6] This observation formed the basis of Mosca's new classification of governments.

In *The Ruling Class* he divided all governments into two types, the feudal and the bureaucratic.[7] In the feudal state the ruling class was simple in structure. Any member of it could exercise economic, judicial, administrative or military functions, and each could exercise direct and personal authority over a member of the ruled class. But in the bureaucratic state these functions were sharply separated from each other and became the exclusive activities of particular sections of the ruling class. Among these sections was a group whose presence gave the bureaucratic state its name. A portion of national wealth was allocated to a body of salaried officials, a bureaucracy.

There were two things in Mosca's analysis well calculated to shock nineteenth-century opinion. His emphasis on the inevitability of minority rule apparently rendered any theory of democracy irrelevant. Secondly, public officials, instead of being regarded as a useful adjunct to a duly constituted sovereign authority, were seen not only as a part of the ruling class in the modern state but as its defining characteristic.[8] For these reasons he has often been regarded as a precursor of Italian fascism. But when we turn to the less read parts of his theory, where he elaborated the place of the bureaucracy in the ruling class, we find that this was far from his intentions.[9]

Mosca was very far from believing that the ruling class had to be monolithic. He rejected the Marxian notion of an identity of interests among those in a similar class position. Instead he made the very possibility of liberty depend upon the differentiation of the ruling class. Where a bureaucracy monopolized wealth and military power he spoke of bureaucratic absolutism. This form of government was 'despotism in its worst form': 'we get a more powerful oligarchy, a more all-embracing "racket", than has ever been seen'.[10] It was essential that a bureaucracy be limited by representative bodies. Through the mechanism of the vote the leaders of different social forces could 'have themselves elected' to such bodies.[11] In this way the ruling class would be a reflection of the varied interests and talents of a society.

Of course, consistent with his programme of analysing politics in realistic terms, Mosca could not afford to be any more sanguine about the operations of parliaments than he was about majority rule. He readily admitted that elected assemblies might not be able to exercise sufficient control upon bureaucracy. Hence, as a further check, he drew upon what he considered to be the lesson of English experience. He called for direct involvement in administration by honorary public servants drawn from both the wealthy and from 'respectable, hard-working people who live in moderate ease'.[12]

Clearly Mosca's innovatory zeal was confined to scientific analysis. The political system he advocated differed little from the blueprints of Mill or Fischel. His importance is not that he differed from nineteenth-century liberals on the need to check bureaucracy but that, agreeing with them on this, he reached the same conclusions on the basis of a different analysis.

None the less it is also true that Mosca's dispassionate method set an example which, followed by others, could easily produce results far more destructive to ideas of representative government than his were. In particular his idea of bureaucracy was susceptible to much more elaboration. He did not feel the need to define bureaucracy, possibly because it does not appear to have meant to him anything more complex than a body of public officials. Whatever had some connection with such a body he called 'bureaucratic'.[13] When he wrote of the 'bureaucratic state' he mentioned characteristics of specialization and centralization which belonged to it, but the essential feature was clearly the use of salaried employees in public services.[14] This apparent crudity was a consequence of what Mosca set out to achieve. He wished to bring discussions of bureaucracy and democracy into the realm of science by neutralizing the terminology, and, to realize this, Mosca aimed at a macroscopic categorization of governments after the fashion of the schemes of Comte and Spencer, which commanded high prestige as examples of social science. In other words Mosca put the concept of bureaucracy into a new context. He brought it from the arena of political argument and offered it as a major category to the still embryonic science of sociology. But he went no further. The first to do so was Robert Michels.

Concerned as he was to examine the implications of his dichotomous classification of governments, Mosca only hinted at the reasons for a bureaucracy's position in the ruling class of a modern state. Michels's *Political Parties* (1911), took up this theme.[15] He agreed with Mosca that a bureaucracy was a necessity in the modern state. In this way the politically dominant classes maintained their position, while the insecure middle classes sought security in state employment. But there was no need to confine analysis to the state if one wished to discover the reasons for the rise of bureaucracies. Implicitly Mosca regarded the state as *sui generis*. However, if one viewed it as an instance of a more embracing category, the organization, and investigated the general features of modern organizational structure, a more fundamental series of reasons could be revealed.

'Who says organization, say oligarchy,' was Michels's aphoristic expression of those fundamental reasons.[16] Drawing his data from the history of political parties, he showed how the leaders of bodies with thousands of members found it necessary to recruit full-time salaried officials. These employees became specialists in various aspects of the organization's requirements. The leaders in their turn required skills and education appropriate for managing a hierarchy of officials. They became a professional leadership, cut off from the general membership by a different cultural background. Naturally the hierarchy of officials depended upon party revenues for their salaries. They therefore avoided any steps which might endanger the size of the membership. Thus, from a means, organization becomes an end.[17]

Salaried officials were not peculiar to the state. Any large organization required them in the modern world. However, Michels not only extended Mosca's thesis to all organizations: he stated it in a more deterministic form. He too reviewed the possibilities of limiting bureaucracy. He considered referenda, syndicalism, and anarchism, but concluded that nothing could withstand 'the iron law of oligarchy'. Perhaps the most that could be expected was that a general consciousness of the oligarchical processes could help to mitigate their rigours.[18]

The determinism of Michels's approach may well have contributed to his showing little more interest in the concept of bureaucracy than Mosca had done. If the salaried official was an inevitable feature of the modern organization, and oligarchy the necessary result, there was little point to analysing the varied forms it might take. The end-product was the same. The simplicity of Mosca's and Michels's concept of bureaucracy—a body of salaried officials —may be seen as the counterpart of their dramatic dismissal of the complex structure of democratic constitutional thought. It facilitated a sociological analysis of the realities of power on a broad and general level. But it was far from the detailed characterization of their contemporary Olszewski,[19] and was only loosely linked with the concepts of power, administration and authority which were an essential part of the analysis. It was Max Weber who took on the huge task of advancing the sociological account of Mosca and Michels, and at the same time doing justice to the high degree of refinement that the concept of bureaucracy had reached in non-sociological literature.

Max Weber: the theory of organization

In terms of the influence it has exerted and the argument it has stimulated Weber's writing on bureaucracy is more important than the sum total of the contributions which have already been discussed. Yet there is a dearth of detailed exposition of his work, as opposed to straightforward borrowing of particular ideas on the one hand, or critical discussions of some fragment of his writing on the other.[20] This is not surprising in view of the variety of versions that he left. Two important sources appeared in his posthumous *Wirtschaft und Gesellschaft* (1921).[21] Apart from them, references to bureaucracy are scattered throughout the two massive volumes of that work. A third vital source, his lengthy essay "Parliament and Government in the Newly-Organized Germany" (1918), has only recently been translated into English and has been unduly neglected.[22]

The results of these difficulties with Weber's text have been paradoxical. He placed more emphasis than any other of the founding fathers of modern sociology upon clarity and coherence of concept-formation. What he wrote about bureaucracy is part of a prodigious effort to codify the concepts of social science. The superficial lucidity of Mosca's and Michels's theses avoided asking vital conceptual questions, such as, 'What do we mean by power, or by administration, authority, the official?' and the many concepts which a discussion of bureaucracy involves. Yet the deeper coherence of Weber's approach, which sprang from asking and offering answers to such questions, has been overshadowed by the dramatic unity of their themes. By contrast, Weber's treatment of bureaucracy has often been considered as a set of isolated *aperçus*. At best it has been seen as the expression of either his general methodology or a philosophy of history.[23]

The remainder of this chapter will offer an exposition of Weber's theory of bureaucracy which emphasizes that it is grounded in a large set of related concepts. In order to let the lines of his argument stand out as clearly as possible the arguments of his many critics will be reserved until the next chapter.

The most relevant conceptual context for such an exposition is to be found in Weber's analysis of organization. In the first chapter of *Wirtschaft und Gesellschaft*, where he examined the basic concepts of sociology, Weber devoted considerable attention to the idea of a *Verband*.[24] This was clearly a concept of very wide significance since it comprised such differing notions as the state, the political party, the church, the sect and the firm. 'Organization' is perhaps the most obvious translation, but in any case *Verband* had a special connotation for Weber.[25] It signified an ordering of social relationships, the maintenance of which certain individuals took as their special task. The presence of a leader and usually also an administrative staff was the defining characteristic of an organization. It was they who preserved the structure. In this remarkably summary manner, Weber incorporated the major point of Mosca's and Michels's analyses. By definition organizations were hierarchic bi- or tri-partite structures.

Weber regarded the fact that human behaviour was regularly oriented to a set of rules (*Ordnung*) as basic to sociological analysis. The existence of a distinctive set of rules governing behaviour was intrinsic to the concept of an organization. Without them it would not be possible to say what was and what was not organizational behaviour. The rules of an organization Weber termed the administrative order (*Verwaltungsordung*).[26] The administrative staff (*Verwaltungsstab*) had a dual relationship to these rules. On the one hand its own behaviour was regulated by them. On the other it had the task of seeing that the rest of the membership adhered to them.[27]

The most important aspect of the administrative order was that it determined who was to give commands to whom. Administration and authority (*Herrschaft*) were intimately linked. 'Every form of authority expresses itself and functions as administration. Every form of administration in some way requires authority, since its direction demands that some sort of power to command is vested in someone.'[28] This is one of the most striking instances of the importance Weber attached to what has also been called imperative co-ordination.[29] Commands and rules ranked as equally important factors in the structuring of social relationships. In an administrative order they were linked in that the rules regulated the scope and possession of authority.

In the Weberian organization with an administrative staff each member was in the position of either giving or receiving orders. The staff both gave and received. It was in this context of examining the basic categories of organizational structure that Weber developed his famous distinction between power (*Macht*) and authority. A person could be said to have power if 'within a social relationship, his own will could be enforced despite resistance'.[30] But such a broad concept, Weber commented, was 'sociologically amorphous'.[31] Individuals could be said to have power in all kinds of ways. For the structuring of human groups it was 'a special instance of power' which was most important.[32] This 'special instance' was authority. It existed when 'a command of a definite content found obedience on the part of specific individuals'.[33]

It cannot be regarded as fortuitous that Weber developed the conceptual distinction between power and authority in the course of his discussion of organizational structure. He made explicit reference to the theory of minority power in organizations in an early essay on authority.[34] But while drawing attention to the factors which favoured oligarchy he stressed that obedience to commands was primarily dependent upon a belief in their legitimacy, a belief that the orders were justified and that it was right to obey. In other words Weber was arguing that it was important not to jump from the facts of orders being given and accepted to the conclusion that those giving the orders had other kinds of power. Interpreted as a gloss on Mosca, Weber was cautioning against automatically regarding every civil servant as a member of the ruling class.

It was the idea of legitimacy which provided Weber with his principle for classifying organizations. In his strongest statement on the subject he said: 'The foundation of all authority, and hence of all compliance with orders, is a belief in prestige, which operates to the advantage of the ruler or rulers.'[35] With different forms of belief in the legitimacy of authority were associated different authority structures and hence organizational forms.

Weber identified three kinds of such beliefs. The first was that obedience was justified because the person giving the order had some sacred or altogether outstanding characteristic. This Weber termed 'charismatic authority'. Secondly, a command might be obeyed out of reverence for old-established patterns of order—'traditional authority'. Thirdly, men might believe that a person giving an order was acting in accordance with his duties as stipulated in a code of legal rules and regulations. This was Weber's category of 'legal authority', which, he added, was of a rational character. It was the type of authority which characterized the modern organization, and with it was associated increasingly a bureaucratic administrative staff.[36]

It was at this point, therefore, among the categories of organizational analysis that the concept of bureaucracy became relevant. It was introduced into an already sharply defined conceptual field. (This was, of course, in turn part of an even more general scheme of concepts for the analysis of social action. It also included more specialized distinctions which would take too long to introduce in this context.)

In a schematic overview of that conceptual field we may distinguish three groups of concepts. First there were the concepts which distinguished between different statuses in the organization, i.e. the leadership, the administrative staff and the general membership. Secondly, there were the concepts which helped to specify the relationship between those statuses, i.e. the administrative order, authority and legitimacy. Finally, the ideas of charisma, tradition and legality were introduced as a means of classifying different authority structures. We must now see how Weber's idea of bureaucracy fitted into this scheme.

Max Weber: the concept of bureaucracy

Weber never defined bureaucracy. This is surprising in two ways. It is regularly assumed that he did make such a definition and his failure to do so is in marked contrast to his efforts to define the other concepts of organizational analysis. Indeed it is clear that Weber did not regard the term 'bureaucracy' as part of the language of social science. It is notable how frequently he enclosed it in quotation marks to indicate that it had been lifted from everyday parlance.[37] What he did take care to do was to specify the features of what he considered the most rational form of bureaucracy. But his general concept of bureaucracy, as opposed to this specific type, must be constructed by inference from the large number of passages where he made allusion to it.

One clue to Weber's general concept is provided by his identification of another kind of bureaucracy apart from the most rational type. This was patrimonial bureaucracy.[38] It differed from the rational type primarily because it depended upon unfree officials rather than contractually appointed men. Weber found examples of this in the later Roman Empire, in ancient Egypt, and in the Byzantine Empire. But clearly intrinsic to the notion of patrimonial bureaucracy was the existence of a body of officials. The concept of an official (*Beamter*) was basic to that of bureaucracy. This is borne out by the frequent occasions on which Weber used *Beamtentum* (officialdom) as an alternative to bureaucracy.[39]

Weber wrote a great deal about the place of the official in modern society. It was for him an increasingly important type of social role. The distinctive features of this role were, first of all, that the individual had specified duties to perform and, secondly, that the facilities and resources necessary for fulfilling those duties were provided by someone other than the role holder. In these respects the official was in the same position as the factory worker, and Weber explicitly referred to Marx's theory of the modern separation of the individual from the means of production.[40] But the official had a characteristic which distinguished him from the worker: he had authority.

Since the official had authority, and, at the same time, this was conferred upon him, it goes almost without saying that an official was involved in administration ('every form of authority expresses itself and functions as administration', see above p. 39). To speak of administrative officials would, for Weber, be pleonastic. But this meant that the concept of an official was bound to comprise many more occupational categories than might at first appear to be the case. The modern army officer, the Roman Catholic bishop, the factory manager were all officials also, spending much of their time in their offices interpreting and transmitting written instructions.

However, Weber did not include all officials within the notion of a bureaucracy. The elected official or the one selected by lot he explicitly refused to call bureaucratic. The essential feature of the bureaucratic official was that he was an appointee.[41] In making this point Weber came his nearest to making a definition of his general usage of bureaucracy. 'No exercise of authority can be purely bureaucratic', he wrote, 'i.e. purely through contractually engaged and appointed officials.'[42]

Perhaps both the technical background and the generality of Weber's concept of bureaucracy can be conveyed in a definition of this kind: by bureaucracy is meant an administrative body of appointed officials. It is noteworthy how close such a formulation is to the concepts of Michels and Mosca. Like them Weber thought of bureaucracy as a collective term for a body of officials, a definite and distinct group whose work and influence could be seen in all kinds of organizations. But it is also true that Weber stressed certain organizational features, in particular appointment procedures, which meant that even in his general concept of bureaucracy were comprised not only the idea of a group but also the notion of distinct forms of action. This became even more important in Weber's concept of the most rational type of bureaucracy.

In spite of the fact that up to this point it has been stressed that Weber had a general concept of bureaucracy, it is none the less true that this was overshadowed in importance, both for him and subsequent commentators, by its so-called rational variant. Indeed to some extent Weber was inconsistent. Sometimes he spoke of bureaucracy in a general and broad sense, at other times he reserved the term for his pure and rational type. A full explanation of this would demand an exploration of Weber's theories of social scientific concept-formation.[43] It may suffice to say that, when faced with a widely disseminated concept of vague outline but broad historical significance, Weber preferred to offer a precise and detailed characterization of the phenomenon as it might appear over a very brief period of time (or, in its complete details, never) rather than to attempt a definition which, in its comprehensiveness, would lack specificity and clarity. This did not, as we have seen, prevent him from writing about bureaucracy in a general sense, especially in polemical contexts.

Weber considered rational bureaucracy as a major element in the rationalization of the modern world, for him the most important of all social processes. Among other things this process involved growing precision and explicitness in the principles governing social organization. This in itself facilitated and encouraged social scientific conceptualization, and the conceptual underpinning of Weber's theory of bureaucracy is at its clearest when he discussed the rational pure type.

In conformity with his theory that a belief in legitimacy was basic to nearly all systems of authority he began by setting out five related beliefs on which legal authority depended.[44] In abbreviated form these were:

I   That a legal code can be established which can claim obedience from members of the organization.

II   That the law is a system of abstract rules which are applied to particular cases, and that administration looks after the interests of the organization within the limits of that law.

III   That the man exercising authority also obeys this impersonal order.

IV   That only *qua* member does the member obey the law.

V   That obedience is due not to the person who holds authority but to the impersonal order which has granted him this position.

On the basis of these conceptions of legitimacy Weber was able to formulate eight propositions about the structuring of legal authority sytems:

(a)   Official tasks are organized on a continuous, regulated basis.

(b)   These tasks are divided into functionally distinct spheres, each furnished with the requisite authority and sanctions.

(c)   Offices are arranged hierarchically, the rights of control and complaint between them being specified.

(d)   The rules according to which work is conducted may be either technical or legal. In both cases trained men are necessary.

(e) The resources of the organization are quite distinct from those of the members as private individuals.

(f) The office holder cannot appropriate his office.

(g) Administration is based on written documents and this tends to make the office (*Bureau*) the hub of the modern organization.

(h) Legal authority systems can take many forms, but are seen at their purest in a bureaucratic administrative staff.[45]

The last proposition is vital for the understanding of Weber's thinking on bureaucracy. The five conceptions of legitimacy and the eight principles of authority were exhibited in the organization of the bureaucratic administrative staff, but they did not in themselves warrant talking of bureaucracy. Other kinds of administration, e.g. collegial or honorary, could also be based on these propositions and Weber discussed them at length (see next section). Weber also added that it was possible to have a bureaucratic administrative staff when the leadership did not base itself on the legal rational principles.

The bureaucractic administrative staff, the bureaucracy in its most rational form, presupposed the preceding propositions on legitimacy and authority, and had the following defining characteristics:

1   The staff members are personally free, observing only the impersonal duties of their offices.

2   There is a clear hierarchy of offices.

3   The functions of the offices are clearly specified.

4   Officials are appointed on the basis of a contract.

5   They are selected on the basis of a professional qualification, ideally substantiated by a diploma gained through examination.

6   They have a money salary, and usually pension rights. The salary is graded according to position in the hierarchy. The official can always leave the post, and under certain circumstances it may also be terminated.

7   The official's post is his sole or major occupation.

8   There is a career structure, and promotion is possible either by seniority or merit, and according to the judgement of superiors.

9   The official may appropriate neither the post nor the resources which go with it.

10 He is subject to a unified control and disciplinary system.[46]

These ten features constituted Max Weber's renowned ideal, pure or most rational type of bureaucracy: the kind of administrative staff which he frequently referred to *tout court* as 'bureaucracy'. Without a doubt the single most important statement on the subject in the social sciences, its influence has been immense. Not only has it blotted out the literature which was discussed in the previous chapter, to a major extent it has dominated its own context in Weber's writing. In the previous section its conceptual foundation was examined. In the next a further specification of the context, where Weber attempted to bind his theory of organization to the theory of democracy will be considered.

Max Weber: the limits on bureaucracy

Weber was sure that rational bureaucracy was bound to increase in importance. It had a series of characteristics—precision, continuity, discipline, strictness, reliability—which made it technically the most satisfactory form of organization, both for authority holders and all other interested parties: 'The development of modern organizational forms in all spheres (state, church, army, party, the economy, interest groups, voluntary associations, charitable bodies or whatever) is simply identical with the development and continuous increase of bureaucratic administration.'[47] On several occasions Weber expressed the view that bureaucratization was an inevitable process.[48] By bureaucratization Weber meant the growth of the ten features he listed as aspects of rational bureaucracy. But as part of the general process of rationalization it tended to imply also the separation of men from the means of production and the general growth of formalism in organizations.[49]

Weber viewed this process with pessimistic resignation but at no point did he coin a term for, nor indeed pay much attention to, the phenomena of red tape and bureaucratic inefficiency which had so preoccupied Olszewski and his predecessors. 'Bureaucratism', which had often been used to designate bureaucratic abuses, Weber used once or twice but without signifying anything more than the special nature of bureaucratic activity.[50] He did not need such a term very frequently since, by defining his bureaucratic administrative staff in terms of organization and duties, when he spoke of bureaucracy the activities of the bureaucrat were implied. But the fact that Weber neglected to examine the inefficiencies of modern administration became, as we shall see in the next chapter, a major debating issue.

However, if Weber minimized the theme of inefficiency, he made up for this by paying close attention to the problem of bureaucratic power. For with bureaucratization went the growth of the power of the officials. It is of great importance to note that this was not a matter of the definition of bureaucratization. That the bureaucrat acquired power was an empirical statement. The sources of this power could be seen in the special knowledge which the official possessed. In the first place he had a specialist's knowledge of disciplines essential to administration in the modern world, e.g. economics or law. Secondly, in the course of his duties he acquired a great deal of concrete information, much of it artificially restricted by ideas of confidentiality and secrecy.

Convinced as he was that bureaucratization was inevitable, and that bureaucrats gained power, none the less Weber resisted any identification of bureaucracy with rule by officials. Indeed it would scarcely be an exaggeration to say that by taking the distinction between power and authority up to the point of insisting that elected officials were not bureaucratic Weber was intent on ensuring that bureaucracy could be analysed without prejudging the issue of the possibility of democracy. De Gournay, Mill and Michels, three very different writers, all represented a school of thought which saw bureaucracy and democracy as opposite and mutually exclusive systems of government. In contrast, Weber's analysis was designed to show that the specific nature of modern administration and the control of the apparatus of the modern state were conceptually distinct.

In spite of the far more highly developed system of concepts, it would be a mistake to infer that Weber was uninterested in the traditional problem of the relation between democracy and bureaucracy. His analytical refinement was not designed to leave this problem behind. On the contrary, his concern for it was the most important motivation behind his interest in bureaucracy. His longest and most important essay in political polemics, "Parliament and Government in the Newly Organized Germany" (1918), was centred upon the problem of *Beamtenherrschaft* in the German state. *Beamtenherrschaft*—rule by officials—was a concept which Weber kept quite distinct from bureaucracy. It was a danger which arose out of bureaucracy and Weber considered it to be realized in the direst form in Germany under Bismarck. He held that Bismarck had enfeebled Germany by allowing officials to occupy decisive positions in the state. The result was a politically stultified nation, with the vigour of the non-bureaucratic classes unable to express itself.

The problem Weber considered was how the inherent tendency of bureaucracy to accumulate power could be prevented from reaching the point where it controlled the policy and action of the organization it was supposed to serve. In this neglected area of his work Weber considered a very large number of mechanisms for limiting the scope of systems of authority generally and bureaucracy in particular.[51] These mechanisms fell into five major categories.

1 Collegiality. The attention Weber paid to this concept provides useful evidence of the extent to which his idea of bureaucracy was influenced by nineteenth-century German administrative theory. Bureaucracy, for him, meant that, at each stage of the official hierarchy, one person, and one person only, had the responsibility for taking a decision. As soon as others were involved in that decision, *as of right*, then the collegial principle was being employed. Weber distinguished twelve forms of collegiality. Among them were included such arrangements as the Roman consulate, the British cabinet, various kinds of senates and parliaments. Weber considered that collegiality would always have an important part to play in limiting bureaucracy, but that its disadvantages in terms of speed of decision and attribution of responsibility meant that it had everywhere receded in the face of the monocratic principle.

2 The Separation of Powers. Bureaucracy involved the division of tasks into relatively distinct functional spheres. Separation of powers meant dividing responsibility for the same function between two or more bodies. For any decision to emerge a compromise between them had to be reached. Weber mentioned the compromise over the budget which historically had to be reached by the British monarch and Parliament. Weber regarded such a system as inherently unstable. One of the authorities was bound to win pre-eminence.

3 *Amateur Administration.* When a government did not pay its administrators it was dependent upon those who had the resources to permit their spending time in unremunerated activity. Such men also had to have sufficient public esteem to command general confidence. This system could not measure up to the demands for expertise which modern society made, and where amateurs were assisted by professionals it was always the latter who made the real decisions.

4 *Direct Democracy.* There were several devices for ensuring that officials were guided directly by, and answerable to, an assembly. Short term of office, selection by lot, permanent possibility of recall were all designed to serve this end. Only in the small organization, as in some forms of local government, was this a feasible method of administration. Here too the need for expertise was a decisive counterweight.

5 *Representation.* The claim of a leader to represent his followers was nothing new. Both charismatic and traditional leaders made such claims. But what was novel in the modern world was the existence of collegial representative bodies, whose members were selected by vote and were free to make decisions and share in authority over those who had elected them. Such a system could not be understood except in relation to the operation of political parties, themselves bureaucratized, but it was through this medium that Weber saw the greatest possibility of a check on bureaucracy.

Weber considered the free parliament in the modern state to be of vital importance in giving expression to the different interest groups which the capitalist economy engendered. Through the party system such groups could find leaders for these assemblies. And in the parliamentary struggle men of real quality, fitted to lead a world power, could be discovered. The Germans did not realize, Weber argued, that the English Parliament acted as a proving ground for political leaders. In important respects Weber's enthusiasm for the representative system owed more to his conviction that national greatness depended on finding able leaders than to any concern for democratic values.[52]

This point is substantiated by the fact that Weber did not regard bureaucratization of political parties as a fundamental obstacle to representative government. On the contrary, the complexity of modern party administration meant that the party leader had acquired essential knowledge of the techniques of modern administration before entering high office. The party leader was not a dilettante. He could exercise real control over state administration. Furthermore the modern party machine demanded discipline and routine. In this way it helped to combat the dangers of demagoguery.

Just as with Mosca, Weber's analysis of bureaucracy led to a plea for adherence to representative government, and for reasons similar to Mosca's. It was not ideally democratic. But it did the most that could be expected under the conditions of modern rationalized society. It steered a middle course between the Scylla of mass irrationality and the Charybdis of bureaucratic tyranny.

3/The Debate with Weber

The sources of Weber's theory

It is not possible to deny the huge advance in sophistication which distinguished Max Weber's theory of bureaucracy from its nineteenth-century predecessors. As we saw in the first chapter, there were several distinct strands in nineteenth-century thinking on bureaucracy. It was Weber's achievement to bring them together. To assess his work in this way appears to cast doubt upon its novelty. But, paradoxically, there was a major element of novelty in Weber's theory which sprang from his neglect of one important aspect of earlier thought. Weber's lack of concern for the problem of bureaucratic inefficiency was in striking contrast to much earlier writing, and has aroused a controversy which goes on today. This chapter will consider that controversy, and will, incidentally, provide an introduction to many of the most important themes in the modern study of bureaucracy.

Before considering his critics' case, it is important to understand the intellectual pedigree of Weber's conceptualizations. It will provide some prior explanation of the imputed defects in his theory and will prepare the ground for the restatement of his position with which this chapter concludes. Unfortunately it is not easy to make precise attributions of influence where Weber's later work is concerned. He rarely bothered with scholarly apparatus and we must rely on indirect internal evidence. However we may detect four major influences. These were German administrative theory; Michels; Marx; and the doyen of German economic and social historians, Gustav Schmoller.

Weber had trained as a lawyer and he wrote a monumental sociology of law. His close acquaintance with German administrative theory, which was a part of a normal legal curriculum, can be taken for granted. It is therefore not surprising that a great deal of his characterization of the ideal type echoed that theory. In particular the clear contrast he drew between monocratic and collegial administration and his balance sheet of their relative advantages and disadvantages could have been found in any administrative text-book from the early nineteenth century onwards (see above, p. 29). Certainly he found there every precedent for viewing state administration as the epitome of efficiency. But it will be recalled that those theorists resisted the application of the label 'bureaucracy' to their models of perfect administration. That he was able to do so without sense of paradox owed something at least to Michels.

Weber's interest in bureaucracy certainly pre-dated the publication of Michels's *Political Parties*. Indeed in 1909, at a conference in Vienna, he caused a considerable storm by the vehemence of his views on the inappropriate extent of the bureaucrats' influence in German society.[1] But he knew Michels well, and they attended the same conferences and informal gatherings. In Michels's work he had a clear link, through Mosca, to the nineteenth-century setting of the problem of the relation between bureaucracy and democracy, and, at the same time, an example of the attempt to treat the issue in a neutral and scientific way. Michels did not want to enter into a harangue against the abuses of officialdom, but at the same time he wished to show the incompatibility of bureaucracy and democracy. It suited him well to adopt as neutral as possible a concept of bureaucracy as a status group of administrative officials, and then to demonstrate ineluctable consequences in the form of concentration of power. It was a way of thinking which Mosca dubbed 'a-democratic' rather than 'anti-democratic'.[2]

Committed as he was to an objective social science, Weber needed the term 'bureaucracy' to serve the same function in his work as it did for Michels. He did not wish to declaim against bureaucracy. Indeed it could be argued that he went in the opposite direction when he stressed its rationality. It was the very rationality of modern administration which raised problems for democracy. The concept of rational bureaucracy (a solecism in terms of nineteenth-century thinking) summed up this issue in the shortest possible way.

In spite of his affinity with Michels, it is hard not to see a note of criticism of that writer in Weber's first essay on bureaucracy. Written in the two years following *Political Parties*, this essay paid especially close attention to the problem of the power position of the bureaucracy. He agreed that bureaucratization was universal in the modern state but argued: 'The fact that bureaucratic organisation is technically the most highly developed means of power in the hands of the man who controls it does not determine the weight that bureaucracy as such is capable of having in a particular social structure.'[3] He likened the argument that the indispensability of the bureaucrat gave him power to the belief that the indispensability of the proletariat necessarily meant it would gain control of the state. 'Whether the power of bureaucracy as such increases cannot be decided *a priori* from such reasons.'[4] As we have already seen, it was just this point which lay at the back of Weber's concern to distinguish power and authority.

A third influence which is clearly visible in Weber's concept of bureaucracy is that of Marx. Weber likened the position of the official, giving orders he did not originate from a room which was not his own, to the position of Marx's expropriated worker, owning nothing but his labour power. It was not what Marx wrote explicitly on bureaucracy which influenced Weber (it was still largely unpublished) but the general thesis on man's alienation which Weber transcended in his theory of rationalization. But in respect of Weber's theory of the development of bureaucracy from its patrimonial to rational forms his debt to Marx should not be over-emphasized. For there was already in existence a developmental account of the growth of administration which was a remarkably precise anticipation of what Weber was to say. This was by Gustav Schmoller.

Schmoller, who had perhaps more prestige as a social and economic scientist than any other of his contemporaries in Germany, was invited to edit and introduce a series of documents on the history of the Prussian administrative system, the *Acta Borussica*. Schmoller wrote a general introduction to this in 1894, and in the same year gave a lecture on German officialdom.[5] These two sources contain a brilliant interpretation of the rise of modern public administration.

Giving credit to Herbert Spencer as his inspiration, Schmoller began from the assumption that every society was constituted of three parts: a leader, his staff and the masses. (As was shown in the previous chapter, Weber's analysis of organization was very similar.) Social development depended on the growing differentiation of these three component parts, while constitutional differences between states stemmed from variations in their relative importance.

As far as the leader's staff was concerned, Schmoller found it possible to distinguish four stages in its development. In the first, in primitive communities, he discerned no genuine differentiation of offices from other roles in society. There followed two stages which overlapped in time. In the one, there were administrative offices filled hereditarily; in the other, offices were of short duration and filled by lot or election. The former characterized feudal societies, the latter was particularly prevalent in classical Greece and Rome. They both depended on a propertied, ruling aristocracy. In the fourth and final stage of development they were replaced by a career structure in which the official was a life-long professional. So that it may be compared directly with Weber's formulation, it is worth letting Schmoller speak for himself on this final stage. It involved:

> a life-long, salaried, professional job for the official, with a clear and fixed career structure for which specialized preparation is necessary. The official is normally appointed by the head of state, and his status, rights and duties are regulated in detail by a developed code of office law. This office structure is the product of an advancing division of labour. As in all earlier civilized nations, it is linked with the formation of social classes. It presupposes an already developed system of offices, which, however, the professional officials radically transform. It is assisted by higher education and the schools which have developed along side of the family. Above all it flourishes as a consequence of a money economy which permits remuneration in the form of salaries for specialized functions, in place of grants of land or support in the lord's household.[6]

Other aspects which Schmoller singled out included the hierarchy of positions and salaries and the fact that it was on the basis of freely signed contracts that men gave their energies to the objectives of the administration. 'This system of offices has, from time to time and in particular states, made great, indeed unsurpassable, achievements, and even where it has not reached unrivalled authority, it has become an indispensable element in the life of the modern state.'[7]

Of course, Schmoller conceded, such a development was not without its darker side. Vom Stein's criticisms were not without content (see above, p. 19). Constant vigilance was necessary to ensure the high quality of officials, and to prevent the dangers of bureaucracy. Quite in accord with the language of those who supported the Prussian state, Schmoller saw bureaucracy as consisting of pathological deviations (of a remediable nature) from the normal course of sound administration.

There was little of a substantive nature for Weber to add to Schmoller's account. His familiarity with it cannot be in doubt. Apart from filling in some of the technical legal detail his main contribution was to recast the conceptual framework. But this was sufficient to give a new direction to thinking about bureaucracy. By identifying bureaucracy with modern officialdom, Weber attempted both to neutralize that contentious concept and to show that the problem of control was inherent in even the most perfect administrative system. By describing such a system as rational he made the ponderous formulations of German administrative theory an expression of a universal historical process.

Even for us, some fifty years after Weber wrote and during which time his influence has been widely felt, some of the paradoxical and self-contradictory overtones of a concept of 'rational bureaucracy' are still apparent. We can be sure they were for him too. The concept summed up his deep ambivalence about the development of modern administration: his admiration for it as an intellectual achievement; his conviction of its inexorable advance; and his fear for its encroachments on individual and national self-expression.

If it was calculated to create controversy, it certainly succeeded. Was the long tradition of writing on bureaucratic inefficiency beside the point? Was Weber's rational type of bureaucracy really as rational as he made it out to be? Was the advance of rationalization so certain? Such issues became the centre of one of the most important themes in modern writing on bureaucracy.

The case against Weber

The simplest stricture of all which could be made against Weber was that he created an unnecessary confusion in vocabulary. As one writer has put it: 'The disadvantages of the application of the words "bureaucracy" and "bureaucratic" to the normal structure of modern administration, as well as to its perversion, are an unnecessary ambiguity and a partial, but incomplete, break with everyday usage . . . his indiscriminate use of the term "bureaucracy" was, therefore, particularly unfortunate.'[8] But, as we have seen, there were compelling reasons for Weber to use this term in spite of (or, indeed, to some extent because of) the break with normal usage. Whether his vocabulary was unfortunate depends on the substantive issue of the cogency of his position. One form of attack on that position has been to question the rationality of Weber's 'rational bureaucracy'.

One of the most well-known essays questioning the idea of rational bureaucracy is a short article by Robert Merton, "Bureaucratic Structure and Personality" (1940).[9] Merton argues that emphasis on precision and reliability in administration may well have self-defeating consequences. Rules, designed as means to ends, may well become ends in themselves. The graded career structure of the bureaucrat may encourage him to an excess of the virtues he is supposed to embody: prudence, discipline, method. Governed by similar work conditions officials develop a group solidarity which may result in opposition to necessary change. Where officials are supposed to serve the public the very norms of impersonality which govern their behaviour may cause conflict with individual citizens.

What Merton is stressing is that a structure which is rational in Weber's sense can easily generate consequences which are unexpected and detrimental to the attainment of an organization's objectives. In so doing he is reasserting, and providing a more sophisticated vindication of, the pre-Weberian view that bureaucracy means inefficiency. (In this respect it is interesting to note that Merton cites Ramsay Muir as one of his sources.[10]) An analogous version of what, in sociological language, Merton terms the dysfunctional consequences of bureaucracy, is provided by the work of Philip Selznick.[11] Concentrating upon the division of functions within an organization, he shows how sub-units set up goals of their own which may conflict with the purposes of the organization as a whole. The remedy for this, the setting up of new departments to counteract the tendencies of the old, only exacerbates the situation by creating more sub-unit goals.

Neither Merton nor Selznick are concerned to point out inconsistencies in Weber's propositions on rational bureaucracy. Rather they intend to show that the formal specification of organizational structure which he outlined is insufficient as a description of how bureaucrats will in fact behave. The official has characteristics as a social being beyond those which the administrative code specifies. Like other men he has interests, prejudices and fears. He forms friendships and cliques. In this respect both Merton and Selznick are applying to administration the major insights derived from industrial sociology of the 1930s.[12] During that time substantial empirical research was demonstrating the importance of informal group processes for morale and productivity in industry.

The internal consistency of Weber's ideal type has been called in question by one of the translators and editors of *Wirtschaft und Gesellschaft*.[13] Talcott Parsons draws attention to the fact that Weber's administrative staff was defined as having professional expertise as well as the right to give orders. Such attributes, argues Parsons, may well give rise to conflict within bureaucracy, since it will be impossible to ensure that high position in the hierarchy of authority will be matched by equivalent professional skill. The problem for members of the organization will then arise of whom to obey, the person with the right to command or the man with the greater expertise.

Parson's criticism is used as a starting point by Alvin Gouldner in his *Patterns of Industrial Bureaucracy* (1955), one of the most important and influential post-Weberian studies. Gouldner generalizes the argument on the conflict of professional and bureaucratic authority into an analysis of the bases of compliance within an organization. He distinguishes two major types of bureaucracy: 'punishment-centred' and 'representative'. In the former, members of the organization conform reluctantly to rules which they consider to be imposed on them by an alien group. But, in the latter, organizational members regard rules as necessary on technical grounds and in their own interests. The two different attitudes to rules have a marked influence on the efficient working of an organization.[14]

An argument similar to that of Gouldner is used by R. G. Francis and R. C. Stone in their *Service and Procedure in Bureaucracy* (1956). They show that, although the official literature of an organization may enjoin impersonality and a strict adherence to fixed procedures, in practice the staff may adapt their action to suit circumstances and the needs of individuals. Gouldner, Francis and Stone, in raising the problem of compliance with rules, are referring, not so much to informal processes arising within an administrative structure, but to conditions outside the organization which determine the members' orientations to the rules and the extent of their consequent implementation.

The view that administrative rationality cannot be assessed out of the context of the culture in which an organization is situated has become a standard item in the criticism of Max Weber, and is one of the earliest critical comments to have been made. In 1928 a distinguished German jurist, Rudolf Smend, complained that Weber was responsible for the misconception that administration was a rational machine, and officials were mere technical functionaries. 'The judge and the administrative official are not *êtres inanimés*. They are cultured (*geistig*), social beings, whose activity has a function within a cultural whole. It is defined by that whole, is oriented towards it, and in return helps to define the nature of that whole.'[15] In the light of this, he added, socialists were on sound ground when they complained of 'bourgeois justice'.

One of the clearest statements of the cultural limitations of administrative rationality is contained in the work of Reinhard Bendix. He argues that the efficiency of an organization cannot be assessed without considering both its formal rules and human attitudes to them.[16] In his *Higher Civil Servants in American Society* (1949) he argues against the belief that it is possible to adhere to a rule without the intrusion of general social and political values. All rules have to be applied to particular cases, and in deciding whether a case falls under a rule the official is called upon to make a judgement. In the exercise of his judgement the official is caught in a dilemma since 'too great a compliance with statutory rules is popularly denounced as bureaucratic. Too great a reliance on initiative, in order to realize the spirit, if not the letter, of the law is popularly denounced as an abuse of power, as interfering with legislative prerogative'.[17]

The demonstration that rules can only be incomplete guides to action not only implies that factors outside the rules must be taken into account by the social scientist in interpreting the action of officials. It also highlights the necessity of choice with which every administrator is faced. It is held against Weber that he appears to permit his bureaucrat to elude all responsibility for his actions. He acts either out of technical necessity or in accord with instructions. Carl Friedrich criticizes Weber for this neglect of the notion of responsibility. He holds that his emphasis on authority 'vibrates with something of the Prussian enthusiasm for the military type of organization, and the way seems barred to any kind of consultative, let alone co-operative pattern'.[18] O. D. Corpuz makes a similar point and argues that responsibility stems from an adherence to attitudes and values which are outside the administrative apparatus.[19]

Both those who, like Merton, delineate the unanticipated consequences of Weberian bureaucracy, and those who, like Bendix, stress that such a structure is contained within a larger society, agree in questioning the rationality and efficiency of Weber's ideal type. Other authors have approached Weber from another direction by asking themselves what, in a given situation, would constitute rational administration, and then have gone on to compare their answers to this question with Weber's own. A good example of such an approach is provided by Peter Blau's *The Dynamics of Bureaucracy* (1955).

Blau considers the work of a United States federal law enforcement agency and a state employment agency. In each he concentrates attention on the way formal regulations are implemented. In the employment agency the central procedures for finding jobs for the unemployed are modified locally in the interests of speedy allocation of jobs. Statistical records of the officials' performance in placing applicants in jobs are designed to permit comparative assessment and encourage competition between officials. Paradoxically, Blau finds that a group of officials who co-operate with each other and pay little attention to such assessments are more productive than those who are stimulated to competitiveness by the records. Even more striking is the way the persistent infringement of a rule in the federal agency actually improves the chances of achieving the agency's goal: the enforcement of two specific laws relating to business finance. Officials who flout the rule that all offers of bribes must be reported find that, by keeping the fact of the offer to themselves (but not the money!), they can ensure that the businessman concerned co-operates fully, out of fear that the attempted bribe will be reported.

The conclusion of Blau's thesis is that a fresh look has to be taken at the concept of rational administration. In a changing environment, 'the stable attainment of organizational objectives depends on perpetual change in the bureaucratic structure'.[20] Therefore efficiency cannot be guaranteed by tethering the official to a set of rigid rules. Only where he is allowed to identify with the purposes of the organization as a whole and to adapt his behaviour to his perception of changing circumstances will efficient administration result.

Similar conclusions to those of Blau have been drawn by A. L. Stinchcombe in an analysis of the American building industry.[21] He argues that the occupational standards of the various craft institutions are the most efficient way of ensuring high quality work. This factor and the great variability in the market in building mean that certain features of Weber's concept of rational bureaucracy, such as continuity of administration, hierarchy and files are not found in the construction industry. A similar argument has been applied to social welfare services. The needs of the poor or the sick are held to demand something other than the Weberian model of administration.[22] Others insist that bureaucracy requires close ties with families and neighbourhoods before it can operate efficiently in the modern community.[23]

Students of non-Western societies offer analogous arguments. Thus R. V. Presthus considers that Weber's concept of bureaucracy makes implicit assumptions about human motivation which are not necessarily valid in non-Western environments. He finds that in the Turkish coal industry, economic and material incentives for effort are not as effective as they would be in the West.[24] W. Delaney considers that patrimonial administration may well be more conducive to economic growth in under-developed societies than rational bureaucracy of the Weberian type.[25] J. La Palombara draws the same inference from a major collection of essays he has edited, *Bureaucracy and Political Development* (1963). He believes that developing societies may find Russian or Chinese methods of administration more effective than Western bureaucracy.[26]

Weber believed that the growth of bureaucracy was inevitable. Its 'rationality' ensured it a place in the general process of rationalization. Clearly this belief becomes questionable when, as with the authors just cited, the very 'rationality' of bureaucracy itself is disputed. But several writers go further and argue that, even if the rationality of Weber's ideal type is granted, this is no warrant for saying that it will always prevail over other administrative systems. Thus Gouldner has criticized the 'metaphysical pathos' of this assumption.[27] H. Constas accuses Weber of taking it for granted that the administrative staff of a charismatic movement will eventually be transformed into a legal bureaucracy.[28] R. Pipes rejects Weber's interpretations of the Russian revolutions of 1905 and 1917 and argues that he was far too impressed by the calibre of the imperial bureaucracy to be able to understand the potential of a revolutionary movement.[29]

It is even suggested by H. G. Creel that Weber was mistaken in seeing rational bureaucracy as a modern phenomenon, and that almost all the characteristics of the ideal type existed in China by 200 B.C.[30] Moreover, irrespective of any consideration of the rationality of the ideal type, many writers consider that Weber erred in seeing it as the necessarily dominant administrative form of the modern world. Thus A. B. Spitzer considers that the functions of the nineteenth-century French prefect are far more comprehensive than those attributed to Weber's bureaucrat and represent a different tradition of administrative organization.[31] M. Berger on Egypt and C. Beck on Eastern Europe also object to the proposition that non-Western administration is necessarily tending in the direction of Weber's ideal type.[32]

One of the results of such criticisms has been a repeated effort to move away from what is regarded as the monolithic nature of Weber's ideal type towards empirical research to find out just which characteristics do distinguish different administrative systems, and which are held in common. The simplest and most forceful statement of this point of view is contained in Carl Friedrich's "Some Observations on Weber's Analysis of Bureaucracy" (1952).[33] He compares the central administrative bodies in England, France, Prussia, the American colonies, and the United States. He finds six characteristics common to them: centralization of control and supervision; differentiation of functions; qualification for office; objectivity; precision and continuity; and secrecy. These features, he concludes, are essential to the concept of bureaucracy.

Since Friedrich's essay several writers have emphasized that the characteristics of Weber's ideal type may each be regarded as a variable. Thus a hierarchy of authority may exist to varying extents in different organizations, and it may or may not be accompanied by selection procedures based on examinations. The inference is drawn that administrative structures should be examined by measuring each of a variety of independently defined dimensions, rather than from the standpoint of a unitary concept of bureaucracy.[34] Such criticisms implicitly question the way Weber arrived at his formulation of the ideal type. Indeed many of the criticisms discussed hitherto can be subsumed under a general criticism of what is taken to be Weber's methodology.

The most succinct statement of the argument against Weber's methodology is contained in Blau and Scott's *Formal Organizations* (1963): 'A careful reading of Weber indicates that he tends to view elements as "bureaucratic" to the extent that they contribute to administrative efficiency. This contribution to efficiency appears to be the criterion of "perfect" embodied in the ideal type. However, whether or not each of these elements, or their combination, enhances administrative efficiency is not a matter for definition; these are questions of fact—hypotheses subject to empirical testing.'[35] In other words, Weber is accused of offering a merely intuitive account of what maximizes administrative efficiency.[36]

We may see that the foundations of such criticism were laid as long ago as 1945 in a modern classic of administrative science, Herbert Simon's *Administrative Behavior*. Without mentioning Weber by name, Simon attacks those theorists who attempt to offer 'timeless' principles of organizational efficiency. Simon argues that different situations require different administrative structures. Hence the theorist's task is best construed as the refinement of the categories of thought appropriate to the diagnosis of administrative situations. In 1958, in his collaborative work with J. G. March and H. Guetskow, *Organisations*, Simon explicitly includes Weber among the exponents of 'timeless' principles of administrative efficiency.[37]

By now the reader can be in no doubt as to the formidable nature of the attack which has been mounted upon Weber's conceptualization of bureaucracy. The rationality of the ideal type is disputed, both because of factors omitted from it, and because of internal inconsistency. The degree of rationality it can have is held to depend on the cultural context in which it is located. If it is accepted that rational bureaucracy is everywhere increasing, then it is held that it must have different features from those which Weber listed. Even if the rationality of Weber's ideal type is accepted, its inevitable growth is disputed. Finally, the very basis on which Weber constructed the ideal type is held to be invalid.

A reply to the critics

If one wishes to sum up the nature of the disagreement between Weber and his critics it can be said that it has two themes. The first is a dispute on the empirical validity (both historical and predictive) of his account of the nature and development of modern administration. The second, and more important, is a rejection of his association of the ideal type of bureaucracy with the concepts of rationality and efficiency. But such a statement of the second theme begs an important question. Indeed, in order to remain as closely as possible to the position of the critics, it was deliberately begged throughout the last section. That question is: 'What did Weber mean by rationality and efficiency, and, in the context of bureaucracy, can those terms be used interchangeably?'

When we turn to Weber's critics we find a general assumption that when he spoke of rationality and bureaucracy, he was talking about efficiency. Certainly most of the writers cited in the last section take it for granted that rationality meant for Weber the suitability of means to a specific end. Thus Francis and Stone say: 'By rationality Weber seems to mean that kind of action or mode of organizing in which goals are clearly conceived and all conduct except that designed to achieve the particular goal is eliminated.'[38] N. Mouzelis strikes a similar note: 'In the Weberian sense, rationality implies the appropriateness of means to ends. In the bureaucratic context this means efficiency.'[39] A German sociologist sympathetic to Weber, Renate Mayntz, argues that the only relevant criticism of the ideal type must focus on the question of whether it reaches maximum efficiency.[40]

This unanimity among the critics is especially surprising because rationality is the most difficult and disputed of all the Weberian concepts. Four major, and several minor variants of the concept occur repeatedly in his work, and they are conflated in his comprehensive developmental idea of rationalization. A general discussion of them would go beyond the scope of this work, but each of the major concepts of rationality appears at some point in Weber's discussions of bureaucracy, and he makes several comments on the specific nature of rationality in a bureaucratic context.[41] It is to these that we turn now.

Considerable time has been spent in showing the close affiliations between Weber's concept of bureaucracy and his other organizational concepts. One facet of these was the link Weber made between the pure type of bureaucracy and legal authority. But it was not, it should be noted, the only form. (He made this clear in the eighth of his propositions on legal authority, see p. 44). This is a more important point than might at first appear to be the case. When Weber spoke of the rationality of legal authority it was not because legal authority was necessarily associated with rational bureaucracy. On the contrary, one of the reasons Weber called bureaucracy rational was because it was a form of legal authority. The problem is thus raised of explaining why Weber attributed rationality to legal authority.

Weber characterized the very conceptions of legitimacy which sustained legal authority as rational.[42] There were three reasons for this. Such conceptions included the idea that both objectives and values could be formulated in a legal code.[43] Secondly, the abstract rules of the code were applied to specific cases, and administration involved the pursuit of interests within that framework.[44] Thirdly, the duties of persons in such a system were limited to specific tasks.[45] Weber called each one of these features rational. We can account for this by considering two elements which appear in each of the three preceding features: the intention in the design of a rule, and the procedure involved in the rule's application.

Weber termed rules 'rational' in so far as their intention was to help the achievement of purposes (technical rules) or to realize values (norms).[46] But the term 'rational' was not only appropriate to rules because of the intention behind them. It could also be used to designate the procedure of applying rules to particular cases. Such a procedure was, for Weber, intrinsically rational. Indeed in the modern world it was becoming increasingly rational, so that it was necessary, both with technical rules and with norms, to employ qualified men with the skill necessary to apply them.[47] It was this kind of rationality which Weber had particularly in mind when he was discussing bureaucracy.

Two separate statements Weber made about the specific nature of the rationality of bureaucracy support such an interpretation: 'Bureaucratic administration signifies authority on the basis of knowledge. This is its specifically rational character';[48] and, 'Bureaucratic authority is specifically rational in the sense of being bound to discursively analysable rules.'[49] Only if one realizes that Weber regarded the implementation of rules in the modern organization as a matter for the expert can one grasp the compatibility of these apparently divergent judgements. This procedure of expert application of rules was central to what Weber called the *formal rationality* of bureaucracy.

It would be quite misleading to equate Weber's concept of formal rationality with the idea of efficiency. It certainly comprised tech-

niques, such as accounting or filing. But it also meant legal expertise, the interpretation of law by lawyers.[50] Administrative action
was not guided by technique alone, but also by norms. Moreover,
Weber frequently referred to the fact that formal rationality did
not guarantee what he called material rationality. Indeed the most
perfect formal system might operate to defeat the purposes and
values which animated it.[51] This was, of course, implicit in his
recognition that bureaucrats might arrogate the highest positions
in the state for themselves.

Formal rationality might be realized in either norms or techniques. But even technical formal rationality did not amount to
efficiency. Certainly it implied calculability, predictability and
stability, but techniques were not in themselves sufficient to achieve
the purposes of an organization. Weber expressed himself vehemently on this point at a conference in Vienna in 1909. No one
denied, he argued, the 'technical superiority of the bureaucratic
machine'.[52] All were agreed that the high morality of the German
bureaucracy contributed to this superiority. But when it came to
comparing the national power position of different countries the
German bureaucracy achieved far less than the corrupt machines
of France and America. 'Which kind of organization has at the
moment the greatest "efficiency" (to use an English expression)—
private capitalistic expansion, linked to a purely business officialdom,
which is more easily open to corruption, or state direction under
the highly moral, enlightened authoritarianism of the German
officialdom?'[53]

This outburst is worthy of note not only because it shows that
Weber was under no illusion that fine technique guaranteed efficiency. It also indicates that 'efficiency' was for him a foreign term.[54]
It appears in many translations of Weber's work but this reflects
more the preconceptions of the translator who cannot conceive of
rationality in the organization except as efficiency, than any consistent usage by Weber of a term equivalent to efficiency.[55] In fact
Weber's concept of formal rationality was more precise and sociologically relevant than any connotation that might be attached to
the notoriously difficult idea of efficiency.[56]

If we define efficiency in a reasonably conventional way as 'the
attainment of a particular goal with the least possible detriment to
other goals', we can see that it corresponds with none of Weber's
categories of rationality. His idea of purposive rationality (*Zweck*

rationalitat) can be seen as comprising efficiency, but it was more than that, involving series of ends and means. The real relation between formal rationality and efficiency can best be understood by considering the means by which efficiency is commonly measured, through the calculation of cost in money terms, or in time, or in energy expended. Such calculations are formal procedures which do not in themselves guarantee efficiency, but are among the conditions for determining what level of efficiency has been reached. At the heart of Weber's idea of formal rationality was the idea of correct calculation, in either numerical terms, as with the accountant, or in logical terms, as with the lawyer. This was normally a necessary though not sufficient condition for the attainment of goals; it could even conflict with material rationality.[57]

Such an interpretation must lead to the rejection of the charge levelled at Weber that he attempted, on an intuitive basis, to state sufficient conditions for the attainment of any organizational goal. Each of the propositions involved in his pure type of bureaucracy referred to a procedure where either legal norms or monetary calculation were involved, and where impersonality and expert knowledge were necessary. Any such procedure was for Weber intrinsically rational, irrespective of its relation to organizational objectives. In short, he was not offering a theory of efficiency, but a statement of the formal procedures which were prevalent in modern administration. In this sense Herbert Simon is quite correct to point to the affinity between Weber's ideal type of bureaucracy and the principles of the classical administrative theorists, but he is quite wrong in assuming that Weber was subscribing to their principles.[58] On the contrary, as a sociologist Weber was recording what happened when men adhered to such theories.

This argument means also that criticism of Weber for neglecting the cultural context of organizations misses the point. Indeed it can be said that Weber was one step ahead of his critics in offering a general theory of modern culture. Where the values and beliefs of a society were informed by logic, calculation and scientific knowledge, where, in other words, the rationalization process had advanced, there, argued Weber, bureaucracy could flourish. Rather than viewing rational bureaucracy as an isolated social phenomenon, Weber made it depend upon other formalized developments, in particular monetary calculation and legal codification.

What do remain open to argument are the empirical validity of

Weber's characterization of modern administration and his predictions of its future development. But the argument must be regarded as evenly balanced. In many ways the formal rationality of modern administration has increased. The features Weber picked out were all exemplified in the Germany of his day. Most of them are true of contemporary civil services. The growth of sciences of decision making, of operational research, of schools of management amounts to an intensification of the importance of science in administration —of formal rationality.[59]

On the other hand, it is undeniably true that he did not see a possible conflict between the growth of formal rules and the application of scientific knowledge. Indeed modern emphasis on the necessity of giving experts a free hand, on flexibility in administration, on job enlargement, on increasing discretion, runs counter to Weber's predictions of ever-increasing formalization. Nor is it wisdom after the event to point this out. Weber's own brother, Alfred, was already writing in 1910 of the need to transform work into a means of personal fulfilment, and was predicting that men would eventually find that the excessively tight bonds of bureaucratic organization were unnecessary.[60]

To conclude, one may say that the novel, unique, and, for later commentators, disturbing feature of Max Weber's account of bureaucracy was his utter disregard for the problems of efficiency. Nor is this surprising. In a theory of the special nature of Western civilization the problems which concerned men such as Olszewski could only appear trivial.[61] Perhaps, given a greater interest in such issues, Weber might have considered the importance Mill had placed upon tradition in maintaining efficiency. He might even have modified the inflexible nature of his predictions to fit his brother's vision. We have seen that he did question the efficiency of German bureaucracy. But, however much he had been concerned with this problem, he would never have needed to retract his view that modern bureaucracy involved *formal* rationality.

4/Bureaucracy and the Ideologists

Max Weber's work was the culmination of the attempt to detach the idea of bureaucracy from the polemical context in which it had emerged. But this did not mean that the concept of bureaucracy was deprived of its place in political controversy. Weber himself attacked the German bureaucracy while, at the same time, attempting to maintain a strict separation between polemics and detached political analysis. Since his time the gap between academic and polemical treatment of the problem of bureaucracy has widened still further. Denunciations of bureaucracy and academic interest in the topic are absorbing the energies of distinct groups of persons, let alone being maintained as separate spheres within the activities of an individual.

In such circumstances some justification for paying even slight attention to the concept of bureaucracy in ideological contexts appears to be necessary. Three reasons can be offered. In the first place, while ideologies are designed to incite men to action this does not mean that their content is wholly emotive. On the contrary, it is a feature of modern ideologies that they purport to be based upon an objective view of the nature of man and society. Secondly, it is notoriously difficult for the social scientist to remove all traces of ideological commitment from his own work, and it is therefore important to be aware of the nature of ideological concepts of bureaucracy. Thirdly, Marxist, and to a lesser extent Fascist, ideologies claim to erase the distinction between ideological and scientific thinking, at least as far as their own doctrines are concerned. Political leaders set themselves up as arbiters of scientific truth and academics avowedly direct their work to political ends. That the scientific element in this conflation of ideology and knowledge cannot be lightly disregarded is obvious when we consider the high prestige as a political scientist which Karl Marx, the most successful ideologist of all time, has in non-Marxist circles.

Karl Marx

In spite of the prolific nature of his writing, Marx made more than passing reference to bureaucracy in one essay only, his first important work after his dissertation, the *Kritik des Hegelschen Staatsrechts*. This was written in 1843, yet, despite its importance it was not published until 1927.[1] In consequence Marxist discussions of bureaucracy depend on inferences drawn from Marx's general political philosophy rather than his specific analysis of the subject. As we shall see such inferences have been fraught with problems, and it could well be that Marx's neglect of the subject stemmed from a perception that his early analysis of bureaucracy fitted badly into his economic interpretation of politics.

Marx introduced the idea of bureaucracy into his criticism of Hegel's conception of the executive powers of the state. In the *Philosophy of Right* (1821), Hegel advanced the view that the state was the vehicle of a general interest distinct from the separate and particular interest of the members of civil society. It was the task of the executive to implement decisions (made by the monarch) about the nature of this general interest. It was shared between collegial advisory committees and state officials and conducted according to the principle of the division of labour, specific duties being allocated to separate departments hierarchically organized under ministers. Since it could not be assumed that any individual was endowed by nature with the ability to execute the general interest, officials had to be specially educated for their task and financially supported so that their personal interests never interfered with the objective fulfilment of their duties.

Hegel singled out two factors for their importance in ensuring that the actions of officials did not exceed the bounds of the general interest. The first was the system of hierarchic authority. The second was the independence of corporations and local communities which embodied the special interests of particular social groups. But, in addition to these formal factors, he held that the values and attitudes of the officials themselves were imbued with a sense of justice and selflessness. The officials made up the most important part of the middle class in which the honesty and intelligence needed by the modern state was concentrated.[2]

Marx's criticism of this account was scathing: Hegel's works did not deserve to be called philosophical exposition, for most of what it had to say could have appeared word for word in the Prussian legal code. He was simply discussing bureaucracy. It is important to note that Marx introduced the term *Bureaucratie* and did not take it from Hegel's text. As one commentator has pointed out, Marx was using it in a pejorative sense.[3] It referred to all the elements in the hierarchical system of administration Hegel outlined, even the collegial advisory boards. In Marx's usage it could refer both to the system of administration and to the men who implemented that system, but more frequently to the latter. If it was the latter he had more in mind he often simply spoke of 'the bureaucrats'.[4]

Marx objected fundamentally to the way Hegel examined the relationship between state and society. In the first place they were separated, the state representing the general interest, society being made up of special interests, and then they were reunited through the devices of hierarchy, independent rights for corporations and the high morality of the official. This appeared to Marx a completely distorted picture. The theoretical opposition between general and special interests was illusory and was used by the bureaucrats to justify their own special interest. Each of the mechanisms Hegel regarded as ensuring the unity of state and society merely evidenced the conflict between the two. The paper qualifications of the bureaucrat were a mark of his separation from the rest of society, the true purposes of the state were submerged in secrecy, mechanistic action, faith in authority and the quest for higher positions in the hierarchy. 'In bureaucracy the identity of the interests of state and of the particular private purpose is so established that the interests of state become a particular private purpose confronting other private purposes.'[5]

Marx agreed with Hegel that the bureaucrats were the main pillar of a middle class, but asked what sort of organization could it have if it depended on a balance of conflicting interests of the officials and other specially privileged groups. The executive power belonged to the whole people and this could only happen when special interest had genuinely become the interest of all.

The section devoted to bureaucracy constituted an important part of the *Kritik des Hegelschen Staatsrechts*. It was a topic on which Marx had clearly thought deeply. But thereafter he scarcely gave it any attention. He made occasional mention of the bureaucrats, but the *Kritik* was neither cited nor published and the Marxist theory of the state developed in independence of it. We must briefly consider Marx's theory of the state if we wish to understand why he allowed the concept of bureaucracy to drop into such an obscure place in his work.

In *The German Ideology* (1846), Marx asserted that although the state had become a separate entity it was 'nothing more than the form of organisation which the bourgeois necessarily adopt . . . for the mutual guarantee of their property and interests'.[6] In the *Manifesto of the Communist Party* (1848), he interpreted political power as 'merely the organised power of one class for oppressing another'.[7] In the *Critique of the Gotha Programme* (1875), he criticized the shallowness of socialist ideas which could not see that existing society was the basis of the existing state and failed to understand that the state was not 'an independent entity that possesses its own intellectual, ethical, and libertarian bases'.[8]

Even where, as in *The German Ideology*, Marx appeared to allow the state a separate identity, he rapidly insisted that this independence was illusory. Throughout his career he attacked liberals, anarchists and socialists alike for believing that either the reform or abolition of the state amounted to a sensible proposition. Since the state depended on the class structure, only a revolution which swept that structure away could effect real political change. He showed particular animosity towards Karl Heinzen, whose study of Prussian bureaucracy appeared two years after Marx's critique of Hegel's position. 'The fatuous Heinzen,' he wrote, 'connecting the existence of classes with the existence of *political* privileges and *monopolies*.'[9]

Could it be that Marx reacted so vehemently against Heinzen precisely because that author had drawn implications from bureaucracy which Marx himself had been perilously near to doing in his own discussion? In it bureaucracy appeared as a near autonomous force, developing its own mode of existence, ruling the rest of society in its own interests.[10] It was a direction of argument which Marx, in developing the idea of the state as the organized power of economically based classes, could not afford to pursue. Bureaucracy had to be seen as an appendage. Any suggestion that the body which merely implemented the formal arrangements of government could become a determining influence on the future of society would have run counter to the belief that nothing could prevent economic forces producing the polarization of society into bourgeoisie and proletariat.

But what sort of appendage was bureaucracy? The insignificant place to which Marx relegated the concept of bureaucracy after his early discussion in the *Kritik* barely concealed the analytical problem with which he was faced. In *The German Ideology* he saw bureaucracy arising in the German states and acquiring abnormal independence because of the inability of any interest group to dominate the others. This transitional stage had persisted in Germany longer than elsewhere, but even so, fundamentally it was the interests of the bourgeoisie which were being served.[11] Yet, only three years later, Marx was saying that the Prussian liberal government of 1848, installed after the March insurrection in Berlin, was representative of the bourgeoisie and had to replace the old bureaucracy 'which does not wish to sink to the level of maidservant to a bourgeoisie to which it was once despotic schoolmistress'.[12]

In *The Eighteenth Brumaire of Louis Bonaparte* (1852), Marx considered that the mass of peasant smallholders in France provided a very suitable base for bureaucracy. With no intermediate grades between it and government direct interference of state power was called forth.[13] Louis Bonaparte was 'forced to create an artificial caste, for which the maintenance of his regime becomes a bread-and-butter question'.[14] This regime was representative of the peasant masses, but at the same time it safeguarded bourgeois order. Not surprisingly Marx noted that this situation was full of 'contradictions'.

Thus, in spite of detecting the existence of bureaucracy in different societies, serving different classes, Marx refused to give it any more than a passing significance. He did not see it as posing any problem for society after the proletarian revolution. In the *Manifesto of the Communist Party*, he envisaged the proletariat centralizing production, credit, means of communication and transport in the hands of the state prior to the 'public power losing its political character'.[15] In *The Civil War in France* (1871), the most important source for his views on the future shape of political power, he assumed that it would be possible for all administrative positions to be filled by election and that their incumbents would be truly responsible to self-governing communes. Since bureaucracy was a class instrument, in a classless society it would not exist—a perhaps not too simple summary of Marx's position.

There can be no question, as is sometimes suggested, that Marx neglected the idea of bureaucracy simply because he was not able, any more than any one else in his time, to foresee twentieth-century developments. His own contemporaries criticized him on this issue. Bakunin, the Russian anarchist who struggled with Marx for control of the International Workingmen's Association, considered that every state was necessarily based upon military and bureaucratic centralization. He criticized Marx and his followers for refusing to see that their ideas were bound to lead to a minority of ex-workers ruling the masses in a powerfully centralized state.[16]

But it was not the anarchists alone who made an issue of bureaucracy. It was a theme which had the unique capacity of uniting conservative, liberal and socialist critics of nineteenth-century social trends. Marx's neglect of it was a pointed effort to dissociate himself from all other ideologies of his time. It affected even remote areas of his historical studies. Karl Wittfogel has shown how Marx's study of Oriental societies was distorted by his refusal to acknowledge that the bureaucracy constituted the ruling class where there was total state power.[17] It was a refusal which was to have dire consequences for later Marxists.

The later Marxists

The lacunae in Marx's account of bureaucracy presented his successors with a double problem. In the first place, they had very little guidance as to how a revolutionary party, and, after a revolution, a socialist state, should be organized. Secondly, once a socialist state had been established the emergence of features in the administrative system which seemed to resemble much which was condemned as bureaucracy in bourgeois states had no easy theoretical explanation. The full brunt of both sides of this problem was met by Lenin. His attempts to resolve the problem met with opposition at every stage.

Lenin's genius resided in his capacity both to organize and to theorize about organization. He was convinced that rational organization was necessary both for winning power and for at least the early stages of a socialist society. At the same time he had to demonstrate his rights to leadership by expounding Marxian ideology. Marx's rejection of bureaucracy as an instrument of class rule clearly hindered him in his organizational task. Before the revolution of 1917 Lenin tried on occasions to eliminate the pejorative connotations of bureaucracy. In 1904 he asserted that a revolutionary party had to be based upon formal, 'bureaucratically' worded rules, and he even called bureaucracy 'the organisational principle of revolutionary Social Democracy'.[18] It was as a result of disputes about such tactics that the split occurred at the party congress of 1903 between Lenin's own group, which became known as the Bolsheviks, and those who were out-voted, the Mensheviks.

But Lenin's insistence upon regulations and discipline was not simply arguable on tactical grounds. Its ideological basis in Marxism was also dubious. The German revisionist leader, Eduard Bernstein, had already warned that the great danger inherent in revolution was the breeding of bureaucracy and he emphasized those aspects of Marx's teaching which implied the necessity for elaborate self-government.[19] Rosa Luxemburg quarrelled directly with Lenin, accusing him of wanting to enslave a young labour movement to an intellectual élite by means of a bureaucratic strait-jacket.[20] She remained of this opinion even after the Russian Revolution. She criticized the lack of freedom of speech, the absence of elections and the right of free assembly. The bureaucracy alone remained as an active element in the state.[21] A different line of attack came from a former ally, Karl Kautsky, who wanted to accept the principle of the inevitability of bureaucratic organization, and wished to re-direct the existing state machinery in the interests of the workers.[22]

Lenin's most ambitious attempt to answer these contradictory criticisms simultaneously was contained in *The State and the Revolution* (1917). On the one hand he asserted that the old state machinery had to be smashed. On the other he insisted on the necessity for strong central control, a dictatorship of the proletariat which would precede the withering away of the state. The burden of his argument was to emphasize that the new form of state instituted after the revolution would be quite distinct from that which went before. There would be government, but it would be in the hands of the armed proletariat. Representative institutions would exist, but not as bourgeois parliamentarianism. They would be Soviets of workers and soldiers deputies. There would be officials, but they would not become bureaucrats, 'i.e., privileged persons divorced from the people and standing *above* the people. That is the *essence* of bureaucracy.'[23]

In order to distinguish his position from Kautsky's, Lenin was forced to refine his idea of bureaucracy. Kautsky had a 'superstitious belief' in it because he failed to understand that, while strict discipline and utmost precision were demanded in all modern organizations, it was not necessary for them to be exercised by appointed officials with power and privilege. So Lenin dissociated his own organizational principles from the idea of bureaucracy, and entrusted their realization to a new, proletarian administrative apparatus. This was to be based on the lessons Marx found in the Paris Commune of 1871. Workers deputies were to supervise the management of the apparatus. They were to be elected, and subject to recall. Their pay was not to exceed a worker's. There was to be 'immediate introduction of control and supervision by *all*, so that *all* may become "bureaucrats" for a time and that, therefore, *nobody* may be able to become a "bureaucrat" '.[24]

If there were any tendencies for proletarian functionaries to become bureaucrats, Lenin attributed them to the corruptive conditions of capitalism. Until the bourgeoisie had been overthrown, there was bound to be some degree of bureaucratization.[25] Small though this reservation was, it took on enormous significance after the revolution. For the issue of bureaucracy rapidly became the focus of the grievances of dissident groups. Under the crisis conditions of the post-revolutionary period, Lenin's programme for proletarian administration was far from being realized. The Ninth Party Congress of 1920 heard scathing attacks on 'bureaucratic centralism'.[26] The Kronstadt sailors' revolt of 1921 listed the bureaucratization of the party as one of the dissidents' major reasons for discontent.[27] At the Tenth Congress, the Workers' Opposition under Alexandra Kollontai demanded a programme of reform which included the expulsion of non-proletarian elements from administration, elections to administrative positions, and the suppression of bureaucracy in the party.[28]

Lenin had to admit that the old state apparatus had not been smashed. At the Eleventh Party Congress he conceded the insufficiencies of Soviet administration, but he would not attribute these to his own organizational principles. Bureaucracy was a survival from the pre-revolutionary period.[29] It was a line to which Stalin tenaciously adhered. In 1925 he admitted that there was a danger of the party losing control of the state apparatus. But this was the result of bourgeois influence, and the state was quite distinct from bourgeois government since it served the interests of the proletariat. In his report to the Sixteenth Congress of the Communist Party in

1930 Stalin conceded that there might even be a new type of Communist bureaucrat who stifled the working class with decrees, and he announced a plan to 'cleanse the apparatus'.[30] In the 1940s the Soviet campaign against bureaucratic tendencies continued in the same vein. Capitalist encirclement and bourgeois survivals were held to contribute to superciliousness and negligence in government and party officials.[31]

Whatever judgement is made on the practicality of the antithesis to bureaucracy which Lenin formulated in *The State and the Revolution*, it did mark an advance in sophistication in Marxist thinking about administration. In the harsh years which followed it was largely ignored. The rules of poverty and recall for officials were abrogated.[32] 'Bureaucracy', instead of being a key term in a theory of administration, became an abusive catchword. Ironically its usage signified an attitude equivalent to that found in nineteenth-century states and heavily criticized by Marx. 'Ultimately, because every state attributes its weaknesses to accidental or intentional defects in administration, it looks to administrative measures to provide the remedy. Why? Precisely because administration is the organising activity of the state.'[33] Marx was arguing that only the destruction of the class system would provide a genuine solution. Stalin was the last person to want to pursue the implications of such a line of thought.

But if, inside Russia, Marxist thinking on bureaucracy was stultified, outside, Marxist opponents of Soviet policy found disturbing theoretical problems in the practices of the Stalinist state. The facts of power in Russia, the fact that the withering away of the state seemed more and more unlikely, appeared to be contrary to some basic tenets, namely: that the sequence of changes through different types of society was determinate; that types of society were deduced from class structure; that politics reflected class structure. How could Russian politics possibly be explained in these terms? The most influential writer to consider this question was Leon Trotsky.

Lenin and Trotsky quarrelled over the latter's criticism of the growth of bureaucracy, and this issue precipitated Trotsky's break with Stalin.[34] In 1924 he criticized the way the party apparatus was imbued with a feeling of its own importance and he lamented that Leninism had become a sacred canon rather than something demanding initiative and ideological courage.[35] In *The Revolution*

Betrayed (1937), he considered the theoretical implications of the emergence of a privileged and commanding stratum in the Soviet Union, the bureaucracy. Trotsky had no doubt that it was legitimate to call the privileged officials of party and government in Russia by the same name as the administrative officials of bourgeois societies. Russian officials were also concerned to maintain a system of social ranks; they too exploited the state for their own ends. But there was a crucial difference. 'The Soviet bureaucracy takes on bourgeois customs without having beside it a national bourgeoisie.'[36]

The crucial question for Marxist theory was whether such a bureaucracy constituted a ruling class. Although Trotsky recognized that it controlled the means of production, he considered that it lacked the essential and distinctive feature of a class: a special type of property. The bureaucracy was, therefore, a stratum or caste, parasitic upon socialist society. Soviet Russia did not require a social revolution, as in 1917, but merely a political revolution which would oust the bureaucracy without changing the basic form of social relations. Hence it was not a new type of society, but was poised between the bourgeois and socialist types.

Trotsky stopped short of a clear break with the orthodox Marxist sequence of societal types. Others were not so timid. A little known work by Bruno Rizzi, *La Bureaucratisation du Monde* (1939), explicitly took issue with Trotsky.[37] Rizzi argued that a new class had arisen in the Soviet Union since the bureaucracy, by paying itself high salaries, became the owner of the surplus value produced by the proletariat. The existence of the new class justified talking of a new type of society which Rizzi designated 'bureaucratic collectivist'. Credit for developing this concept was also claimed by Max Schachtman, editor of *The New International*, who, in a series of articles in that journal from 1940 onwards, rejected the notion that the Soviet Union was either socialist or capitalist.[38]

Schachtman disagreed with those who thought modern societies were converging to a managerial type. He thus indicated his independence from a line of thought of which Rizzi was an early exponent. For the latter found that the United States and Fascist societies were equally dominated by professional specialists and technicians.[39] All developed societies were approaching an identical destiny and Marxists were deluded in thinking that the proletariat could ever obtain power without generating bureaucracy. None the less Rizzi believed that the skill of the bureaucrats would eventually raise the material conditions of life to the point where the gap between them and the working classes would be minimal.[40] Such an approach, which emphasized the role of specialist knowledge in both government and the economy, highlighted specific features of the twentieth century which necessarily strained traditional Marxist analysis.

The most celebrated and most radical departure from that analysis came in 1957 with the publication of *The New Class* by Milovan Djilas, former vice-president of Yugoslavia. It is well known that this book occasioned a seven-year prison sentence, but its theoretical significance has been neglected. At point after point Djilas breaks with basic Marxist tenets. Communist states are run by the party. The party is a bureaucracy. The bureaucracy is a class since it uses and disposes of state property. But it also depends on two other equally important factors; force and ideological dogmatism. It needs these to secure its power precisely because it is not firmly embedded in the socio-economic order. It is not a transitional phenomenon, but part of a special type of state system. This system will develop in separate national directions.

Certainly the mere fact of an attack on bureaucracy did not endanger Djilas. In 1949 and 1950 Tito was leading attacks on the Soviet state system and criticizing Stalin for bureaucratic tendencies. A programme was implemented to secure decentralization and control at all levels by people's committees.[41] But, as I. Lapenna pointed out, the place of the conception of bureaucracy in Soviet and Yugoslav theory did not vary greatly.[42] In both cases attention was concentrated on what were seen to be remediable administrative abuses, even though the practical measures differed. Djilas's attack was designed to subvert the whole Communist theory of the state. It was more dangerous by far than a programme of administrative reform.

Outside Europe, where revolutionary movements with a Marxist ideology have taken control, the same ambivalences towards the idea of bureaucracy as appeared in the Soviet Union are apt to recur. Mao Tse-tung regularly fuses the ideas of bureaucracy and capitalism and attacks 'bureaucrat-capitalists'.[43] He also refers to the dangers of bureaucracy in the Communist Party, but he warns against equating counter-revolutionary bureaucracy with the revolutionary form, which is a correctable malady. Similarly, in Cuba

Castro has attacked the socialist bureaucrats in his own agencies. But, as a sympathetic outsider, René Dumont, has commented, the Cuban leaders regard bureaucratic tendencies as a mysterious disease, cause unknown.[44] For the more romantic 'Che' Guevara such issues were merely 'quantitative' and ultimately of little importance.[45]

Only in the last few years, with the rise of the diffuse movement known as the New Left, has the concept of bureaucracy come to take a major place in doctrine which claims to stem from Marx. Lichtheim has pointed out that the Hungarian rising of 1956 secured the admission from critically minded Marxists that bureaucracy was the central problem for the new society.[46] The spokesmen of the Paris student revolt of May, 1968, bear out this judgement. One of them goes as far as to define socialism as 'a rejection of all bureaucracy, of all centralized direction, by granting power to the producers at their point of production'.[47] But their idea of bureaucracy is more all-embracing than that of even the early Marx. It appears to comprise hierarchy, specialization, authority and alienation. Such a concept is derived as much from the multiple-factor approach of modern sociology as from Marx, and so acute is the consciousness of the Procrustean nature of modern organization that any structuring of the student movement is rejected for fear of the taint of bureaucracy.[48]

Probably a turning point in left-wing ideology has been reached. More conventional Marxists of the New Left, for instance those who contributed to the *May Day Manifesto 1968*, may avoid a full confrontation with the problem of bureaucracy, but the student activists in France or the United States have made organizational structure, rather than the class system, their main target.[49] The systematization of these ideas requires an ideologist with as much knowledge of modern social and political science as Marx had of bourgeois philosophy and economics. Kautsky and Djilas are merely notable exceptions to the rule that, hitherto, Marxists have shunned Western social science.[50]

Whether such an ideological synthesis would generate new political forms is an issue which cannot be pursued here. But it is noteworthy that a theoretical dispute over bureaucracy has so often been the ostensible reason for many famous partings of the way in the Communist world—between the Bolsheviks and Mensheviks, Trotsky and Stalin, Stalin and Tito, Tito and Djilas. An ideology with a developed doctrine of bureaucracy would at least be spared an obvious pretext for schism. In this respect, Fascism provides an instructive example.

The Fascists

As opposed to the Marxists, the Fascists not only put a theory of the state at the centre of their doctrine, they also sought to resolve the problem of the relation of the individual to the state by asserting the identity of their interests. Authority, hierarchy, obedience were extolled, and even if attempts were made to capitalize on the unpopularity of civil servants, Fascists were too intent on capturing the state intact and using it for their own ends to be able to afford to alienate its instruments. Their ideology was, therefore, unique in its response to bureaucracy. It was not considered to present any problem, and the term itself lost any pejorative connotations.[51]

However, in comparison with Marxism, Fascist ideology was a largely *ad hoc* collection of ideas assembled for opportunistic reasons.[52] It was, therefore, conditioned very directly by the circumstances in which its was conceived, and it would be wrong to neglect the differing emphases placed on the idea of bureaucracy in Italy and Germany. The Italian Fascists had the problem of fostering greater docility to state interference, while the Nazis had to re-direct an already highly developed state machine. Hence for Mussolini: 'It is not the nation which generates the State . . . rather it is the State which creates the nation',[53] while for Hitler, 'the State is not an end but a means', drawing its strength from the nation and merely helping to promote its development.[54]

Mussolini made a point of praising the Italian state officials as often as possible. In a speech in 1924 he said that the bureaucracy alone had prevented chaos in Italy.[55] In his autobiography he asserted: 'All that is just, finds in the Italian bureaucracy an immediate comprehension.'[56] In a speech on the corporate state, in 1933, he denied that bureaucracy was any barrier between the people and the state since, under Fascism, the citizen was intimately associated with the administrative machinery.[57] Mussolini admired the machinery of state because it was on similar principles that he had built his own party, and the society he envisaged was to be based on interlocking hierarchies.[58] He saw bureaucracy simply as a body of officials or the method of modern administration, a fact of modern life to be taken for granted. It was a formulation strikingly similar to that of his admirer, Michels. Only when he spoke of bureaucratization, the freezing of the economy under communism, did a disparaging tone enter his comments.[59]

The idea of bureaucracy had an insignificant place in Nazi writing. Hitler asserted that his movement would put life in a machine when he spoke of the civil service of the Weimar Republic, but he expressed admiration for the competence and incorruptibility of the civil service of the empire.[60] He could not afford to disparage the force, which, next to the army, was the most powerful in the state. At the same time, when he came to power he tried to ensure its subservience to himself by subjecting it to Nazi supervision and infiltration. The consequences of this have frequently been analysed by later commentators, but at the time ideological justification was perfunctory.[61] Alfred Rosenberg wrote once or twice of the way German officialdom had been brought out of the bureaucrat's office and given back to the people, but the Nazis felt little need of any more elaborate theory.[62]

The fact that a dispassionate concept of bureaucracy as an instrument of the state was held both in Fascist thought and in the theories of the classical writers, and the fact that these were the productions of the same two countries, could occasion an oversimple linking of the two sets of ideas. In the case of Michels a link can be made, but to say that, by analogy, the link must be there also between Weber and Nazism would be to neglect the specific features of the Nazi ideology. For it is clear from a leading academic sympathizer with Hitler, Carl Schmitt, that Weber's idea of bureaucracy could not appeal to a movement which claimed to revitalize the nation. Hitler needed the bureaucracy as an instrument but also as a political ally prepared to intervene in national life in a direct way on his behalf. Weber, argued Schmitt, neglected the role of bureaucracies as élites and carriers of values and could only see them as purely technical bodies.[63]

If the Nazis supported bureaucracy it was because they saw in it an élite group prepared to assist them in exercising power. For them and the Italian Fascists this represented the intimate union of nation and state. It is precisely these connotations of bureaucracy, a privileged élite group claiming to represent national interests, which has been the target of ideologists committed to Western representative institutions.

The ideologists of representative democracy

A good illustration of the limitations of the concepts of right and left wing is provided by the attitudes of Western conservatives and socialists towards bureaucracy. Although those who do not wish to see existing social inequalities undermined might be considered to be on the same wing as the Fascists, their views on bureaucracy are diametrically opposite. Similarly the socialist' committed to Western representative institutions tends to accept bureaucracy as a fact of modern life and does not share the Marxist's antipathy towards it.

In the United States especially, and to a lesser extent in Britain, conservatism has been associated with opposition to governmental intervention, and it has become customary to attack all such activity as bureaucracy. A large literature exists which singles out for attack specific features of government and labels them 'bureaucracy'.[64] Such features may be the proliferation of regulations or the opposite, the bestowal of discretion upon the official, or nationalization, or officials who behave obnoxiously, or sometimes simply socialism. Herring has commented on this genre of writing and its use of the concept of bureaucracy. He argues that 'bureaucracy' has become an emotional stereotype meaning only 'that-aspect-of-administration-which-is-disliked-by-those-who-are-adversely-affected'.[65]

The nearest approach to a measured exposition of the conservative concept of bureaucracy is in the work of Ludwig von Mises. Arguing that the term always has opprobrious connotations he asserts that 'nobody has ever tried to determine in unambiguous language what bureaucracy really means'.[66] This comment is a good illustration of the intellectual isolation of the exponents of this concept of bureaucracy. Von Mises ignores virtually all the previous literature on bureaucracy—and understandably so—since he tries to show that inefficiency is of the essence of governmental intervention, and that it is only governmental inefficiency which deserves the name of bureaucracy. Indeed he argues that private enterprise only shows the traits of bureaucracy as a result of public interference. Bureaucracy is the antithesis of business motivated by the desire for profit. It is the same conflict as that between capitalism and socialism.

Von Mises is both attacking socialists and trying to forestall their customary rejoinder, which is that all modern organizations, public or private, show essentially the same traits. Socialists reject the concept of bureaucracy as governmental interference and react with some degree of fatalism to what they regard as the universal features of modern organization: size, impersonality, regulation. Thus Schumpeter confesses: 'I for one cannot visualize, in the conditions of modern society, a socialist organization in any form other than that of a huge and all embracing bureaucratic apparatus. Every other possibility I can conceive would spell failure and breakdown.'[67] But he goes on to argue that bureaucracy affects every sphere of life, and that it is a necessary complement of modern democracy.

Schumpeter also suggests the conditions under which bureaucracy can work to the advantage of democracy. But such concern for this problem is rare among socialists.[68] Normally it is mentioned in passing only. Among British Labour Party politicians only Richard Crossman has shown a consistent desire to specify the mechanisms which could abate the problems of a swelling civil service, the concentration of power in public and private corporations, the growing independence of the civil servant. His collection of essays, *Planning for Freedom* (1965), emphasizes the necessity of power with responsibility, the need for Parliamentary committees, and further constitutional safeguards for individual citizens.

The only group in recent British politics which has attempted to make bureaucracy a central issue of controversy has been the Liberal Party. It has advocated workers' control in industry and called for the devolution of government functions. Its former leader, Jo Grimond, has expressed admiration for Yugoslav reforms of the last decade, and in many respects the party has pursued a line of thought very similar to that of the more unorthodox Marxists of the New Left. In both cases the concept of bureaucracy embraces the whole area of contact between individual and organization. In Grimond's words: 'In saying that our system is "bureaucratic" I mean primarily that decisions tend to be taken by the pressure of various organizations acting in the interests of their own apparatus. Anyone outside an organization is of little importance.'[69]

As we shall see, the preoccupations of the British Liberals run approximately parallel to those of many contemporary political scientists. Yet it is difficult to conceal the fact that the total fund of ideas on bureaucracy possessed by Western politicians seems sparse, even when compared with the Marxists'. This must be attributed to the very division of labour between scientist and politician which the Marxist aims to abolish. It is a presupposition of the ideology of representative democracy that the academic study of political life can be pursued without endangering, indeed even without relevance to, accepted political institutions.

But the idea of bureaucracy has rarely been divorced from the feeling that it involves practical problems which demand solutions. Many Western academics do conceive it as their task to offer 'solutions' to the problem of bureaucracy. They aim to act as brokers between the politician and the scientist, interpreting the meaning of democracy for the latter, giving the facts to the former. They may, perhaps, be viewed as the real ideologists and we shall consider them in chapter 6. Before that we must turn to that peculiar product of the West, the continuing attempt to develop an objective, dispassionate, detached account of a controversial political topic—in short, social science.

5/ Seven Modern Concepts of Bureaucracy

It is possible a reader will turn with relief to this chapter, hoping that the plethora of competing concepts previously detailed will finally be clarified and organized. He may have interpreted the purpose of the earlier chapters as the provision of a backcloth to definitive achievements by the present generation of scholars. But if so, he will be disappointed. For, as the mention of seven concepts of bureaucracy implies, modern endeavour in the social sciences has led to a further proliferation of concepts. Sophistication in argument and research has not resolved old problems, but merely elaborated them, and the relation of the earlier chapters to this one is more in the nature of an explanation of the basic positions from which modern argument stems than a foretaste of better things to come.

As with any argument, if one comes in at a late stage a prerequisite for understanding how that stage has been reached is to retrace the course of discussion, and this is true even if those who are arguing are no longer aware of how they have reached their present positions. In this way, some sense can be found in a situation where literally hundreds of definitions of bureaucracy compete and where the differences between them amount to more than minor verbal discrepancies. For this reason modern concepts of bureaucracy will be classified here according to their historical and logical affiliations with the concepts which have already been examined. Such a procedure recommends itself all the more clearly since it has already been followed, and in part completed, in respect of the continuing debates with Weber and within Marxism. Only in this way can any thematic unity behind modern concepts of bureaucracy be discerned.

The discussion in this chapter does not follow the only possible mode of presentation. Several alternative modes present themselves. If one wished to highlight the fragmentation of the literature it would be sufficient to present concepts of bureaucracy according to the disciplinary affiliation of the authors. Historians, political scientists, economists, management scientists, sociologists and social psychologists have, in general, preferred to discuss differing concepts of bureaucracy within their own discipline rather than to seek for similar concepts in other disciplines.

It would also be possible to consider concepts of bureaucracy according to the types of general propositions with which they might be associated. Bureaucracy has normally been a term in a wide variety of theories about modern society. It has been linked with the growth of tertiary occupations, with the differentiation of social functions, with the alienation of man from work, with the growth of oligarchy and with a general process of rationalization. It has been an element in many more restricted theories about rules, hierarchy, communication, participation and decision making in a wide variety of organizations. But there has been no consistent linking of particular concepts of bureaucracy with particular theories. Thus, while some theorists may agree on employing the concept of bureaucracy in the sense of the power of officials, they are quite likely to disagree on whether the growth of such power is to be anticipated in industrialized societies. Others may agree that the growth of formal regulations is likely to hinder free communication but disagree as to whether such formal regulation is to be called bureaucracy. Another possibility is that ostensibly similar propositions may be advanced: e.g. that bureaucracy increases the likelihood of alienation from work, when in one case a writer is taking bureaucracy to mean a rational system of organization, and in another case administrative inefficiency is what is meant.

This does not amount to saying that the choice of concept has no implications at all for the kind of theories a social scientist may advance. We have seen, for instance, how the concepts of bureaucracy held by Mosca, Michels and Weber were part of a conceptual frame of reference which tended to exclude the possibility of formulating generalizations about administrative inefficiency. We shall note such limiting tendencies again. But to view concepts primarily from the standpoint of the theories of which they form elements, or, indeed, of the disciplines in which they have been elaborated, would involve separate analyses of the development of those theories or disciplines.

The same might be said of a third way in which the ensuing discussion might be organized; that is, according to the conceptual strategy which the various writers have employed. The very fact of variety among concepts of bureaucracy confronts social scientists with the necessity of choice. Moreover most would feel that this has to be an argued choice, even if the argument only amounts to showing that the decision for one or the other concept is arbitrary. We shall meet the occasional writer who seems unaware that anyone has ever found the concept of bureaucracy problematical, but this is rare.[1] The procedure which is adopted in coming to a decision as to which concept to prefer may conveniently be called a conceptual strategy.

There is a wide variety of such strategies. It is possible to gather a range of definitions of bureaucracy and then attempt to find some common factor in them. An effort may be made to find some kind of majority opinion. The writer may seek to consider the objects (*denotata*) to which the term has been applied and then offer a new definition. Various criteria may be advanced to justify the adoption of an existing definition, e.g. compatibility with colloquial speech, or use by an authoritative figure, or place in an influential theory. A case may be made out for offering a new definition of the writer's own simply in the interests of clarity. A definition may be chosen which facilitates measurement and field work.

Each of these strategies is represented in the discussion of the concept of bureaucracy, and attention will be drawn to them in the following pages.[2] But these strategies stem, not from the tradition of writing about bureaucracy, but from a writer's general position on the methodology of social science. They cannot, therefore, be used to organize the material of this chapter without blurring the continuities of writing which it has been the task of this book to document. To preserve this developmental perspective modern writing on bureaucracy will be reviewed by taking in turn the concepts with which we are already familiar, referring to the various disciplinary affiliations, theoretical inclinations and conceptual strategies of the authors only when this will be of assistance in explaining any deviations from, or elaborations of, the established meanings of bureaucracy.

But before beginning that task we should briefly notice one conceptual strategy which simply involves accepting as authoritative the concept of bureaucracy which Max Weber formulated. Such an approach clearly recommends itself to writers of textbooks, but it has also been employed in more notable publications such as

Mouzelis's *Organization and Bureaucracy* and Nettl's *Political Mobilization*.[3] At first sight no other method might appear to preserve a concept so well and permit research to proceed with less sterile conceptual discussion. But of course this is to neglect the difficulties which subsequent commentators have found in interpreting Weber's concept and to leave us unenlightened as to which of the many interpretations is being accepted. Thus we are normally left to assume that it is the ideal type which is being adopted and not Weber's more general concept.[4] When an interpretation of Weber's concept is offered, then it will normally fall within one of the major categories we shall now consider.[5]

1/ Bureaucracy as rational organization

We have seen that the most difficult problem commentators on Max Weber have found has been to understand the relation between his idea of rationality and the specific characteristics he attributed to the ideal type of bureaucracy. It has become customary to argue that there is no necessary relationship between these characteristics and rationality, and from this the inference has been drawn that there are two alternative ways of conceptualizing bureaucracy. (We have also shown that this problem has largely been of the commentators' own making, but this is immaterial in this context.)

The most eloquent exponent of this point of view has been Peter Blau. 'Weber conceived of bureaucracy as a social mechanism that maximizes efficiency and also as a form of social organization with specific characteristics. Both these criteria cannot be part of the definition, since the relationship between the attributes of a social institution and its consequences is a question for empirical verification and not a matter of definition.'[6] Having identified these alternatives Blau has oscillated between them in his own work. In *Bureaucracy in Modern Society* (1956), he suggests that it might be preferable to define bureaucracy as 'organization that maximizes efficiency in administration'.[7] But in the book he co-authored with W. Richard Scott, *Formal Organizations* (1963), he considers that the term 'is used neutrally to refer to the administrative aspects of organizations'.[8]

Other sociologists have been less prone to doubt. Francis and Stone state that technically 'the term bureaucracy refers to that mode of organizing which is peculiarly well adapted to maintaining stability and efficiency in organizations that are large and complex'.[9] The fact that this concept appears to have the authority of Weber's name behind it has meant that it has acquired increasing popularity in the last decade. As a typical example we may cite Peter Leonard's definition: 'It simply refers to the rational and clearly defined arrangement of activities which are directed towards fulfilling the purposes of the organization.'[10] The consequence has been a situation which it would be hard to parallel for apparent perversity. The sociologist is forced to admit that his idea of bureaucracy is diametrically opposed to the popular concept of bureaucracy as administrative inefficiency. As a justification he normally points to the value-laden aspect of the popular idea, his own concept being purely 'technical' or 'neutral'.[11] The reader is left to infer that somehow judgements on inefficiency are evaluative while those on efficiency are value-free.

It is not surprising that this concept of bureaucracy, although developed by sociologists, has appealed to management theorists since the idea of efficiency has been central to much of their writing.[12] But this observation immediately highlights the nature of this concept. Herbert Simon has stressed the heuristic and normative use of the idea of rationality and has pointed out that it is not possible to stipulate any determinate procedures which invariably realize the ideal of organizational efficiency. This does not only mean that research into rational organization in different societies is bound to find many organizational forms.[13] To claim to establish what is rational in any situation is to purport to arbitrate on the principles which the participants in that situation are applying. It means very often the erection of new principles to replace those the observer discerns. Thus Blau's *Dynamics of Bureaucracy* proposes to revise the concept of rational administration and advocates certain practices which will ensure 'the stable attainment of organizational objectives'.[14] Paradoxically, the assertion of the relativity of standards of rationality is only the prelude to offering a more universally applicable set.

The point at issue here is an illustration of what is involved in any sociological definition of an institution which has its own codes of rules. The sociologist of law, for instance, does not claim to elaborate or adjudicate on legal principles. He does not attempt to define law as 'that which accords with the principles of justice', but rather adopts an outsider's position and studies those situations where men have applied rules which they call law. This position is open also to the sociologist of organizations.[15] There is a major distinction to be drawn between defining bureaucracy as 'rational organization' and as 'organization where men apply criteria of rationality to their action'. The latter corresponds much more closely with the spirit of Weber's ideal type. But it is a distinction which is not normally made, and until it is this concept of bureaucracy must be seen as belonging to the same logical category as the concept which has so frequently been spurned as 'popular', organizational inefficiency.[16]

2/ Bureaucracy as organizational inefficiency

We saw how, in the nineteenth century, it was customary to comment on the pejorative overtones which the term bureaucracy had in everyday language. The concept of bureaucracy as rational organization has always been the property of an academic élite, and we can trace this idea back to the German administrative theorists of the nineteenth century entirely through academic publications. But the concept of bureaucracy as inefficient organization has needed no scholarly tradition to sustain it. Moreover, those scholars who favour this concept have tended to justify it by reference to popular usage rather than by seeking academic authority. At least this is so where the idea of inefficiency does not extend to comprising the arrogation of power by officials, a concept with the whole tradition of political theory behind it and which will be considered later in this chapter.

The result is that this concept of organizational inefficiency makes frequent but isolated appearances in the literature of social science. Among management theorists Marshall Dimock in particular has used the concept of bureaucracy as the antithesis of administrative vitality and managerial creativity. It is defined as 'the composite institutional manifestations which tend towards inflexibility and depersonalisation'.[17] He attributes its growth to a wide variety of factors including organizational size, the proliferation of rules, group introversion, and too great an emphasis on age and security. Among writers on politics a concept similar to that of Dimock's, though independently developed, is held by E. Strauss. In *The Ruling Servants* (1961), he reserves the term bureaucracy for 'the many imperfections in the structure and functioning of big organizations'.[18] Symptoms of bureaucracy include over-devotion to precedent, lack of initiative, procrastination, proliferation of forms, duplication of effort and departmentalism.

While there may be at most a broken intellectual tradition to justify labelling organizational inefficiency as bureaucracy, it is of course true that writers on bureaucracy and rationality have provided a theoretical framework for discussing inefficiency. Chapter 3 discussed how many commentators on Weber, among whom Merton is the most notable, have shown how informal and unanticipated processes, generated by ostensibly rational organization, may occasion administrative delay and public complaints of red tape. For many writers this has meant jettisoning the concept of bureaucracy as rational organization, and inceed discarding the implicit normative orientation involved in the concept of rationality. But a recent French representative of this largely American tradition of writing, Michel Crozier, has crossed to the opposite side and, like Dimock and Strauss, sees bureaucracy as essentially inefficient organization.

In *The Bureaucratic Phenomenon* (1964), Crozier sees bureaucracy as 'an organization that cannot correct its behavior by learning from its errors'.[19] He shows how the rules of an organization may be used by the individuals within it to their own advantage, and how, in consequence, the interest which various strata have in preserving the status quo produces rigidity of structure. Such a system, Crozier argues, is badly adapted to the needs of modern business and technology. But the moment this is said the normative orientation of this concept of bureaucracy is apparent. The fact that Crozier and Blau contradict each other on the usage of the term bureaucracy cannot hide their commitment to very similar concepts of organizational rationality. Each places a high value on flexibility and adaptability.[20]

Whether this commitment is regrettable or laudable is, in this context, beside the point. But it is striking how much Crozier's analysis reflects his own dissatisfaction with French organizational structure rather than registers the complaints of the participants in the situation. Indeed, he acknowledges that they derive multiple satisfactions from it. As with the previous concept, clarity would be enhanced by distinguishing between inefficiency as discerned by the analyst in applying his own criteria and the situation which arouses complaints of bureaucracy among a public. It is worth noting that this distinction is provided for in the German literature by employing both the term *Bürokratismus* and *Bürokratie*. The former usually refers to an ethos of officialdom which antagonizes the public.[21]

3/ Bureaucracy as rule by officials

The problem of normative orientation, inherent in the two previously considered concepts, is of course at the forefront again when we turn to what can claim to be the original concept of bureaucracy: rule by officials. It was in this sense that de Gournay and Mill used the term, and we have seen how this was a deliberate elaboration of the classical framework of thought about types of government. But, in spite of this origin in traditional political theory, this concept has been markedly less subject to the amalgamation of positive and normative standpoints than the concepts we have just discussed.

This ought not to be too surprising. The Greek concepts originated as much in the desire to classify as to criticize, and to a large extent it is the modern treatment of one particular concept of the classical framework—democracy—which has led to a widespread assumption that it is ill-adapted to social scientific requirements. It is the modern wish to view democracy not in terms of the rule of a class but as rule for the good of the whole people, and here clearly the normative argument begins. It means that, whatever the distribution of power (and it is always unevenly distributed), efforts will be made to show that true democracy exists. Hence bureaucracy may be shown to be compatible with, or even necessary to, democracy, and this issue has loomed so large that the next chapter will be devoted to it. But if the question being asked is simply 'Who has power?' rather than 'Whom does power benefit?' then the concepts of bureaucracy, monarchy or aristocracy can be seen as specifications of the nature of the group or individual who at any time holds power.

In spite of its relative antiquity, the line of thought which has maintained the idea of bureaucracy as the rule of officials has been extremely tenuous. This is partly due to the overwhelming amount of attention which has been paid to the idea of bureaucracy as rational organization. But it is also attributable to the unfashionable nature of comprehensive schemes of classification in Western political thought: such a degree of systematization is normally deemed to be characteristic of Marxism and deterministic thinking in general. (We have examined in detail why the notion of officials as a ruling group has been anathema to Marxists, at least until the heresies of Rizzi and Djilas.)

However, between the two world wars, there was a sufficient number of notable thinkers to maintain the original concept of bureaucracy. An influential definition was that of Harold Laski in the *Encyclopaedia of the Social Sciences* (1930): 'Bureaucracy is the term usually applied to a system of government the control of which is so completely in the hands of officials that their power jeopardises the liberties of ordinary citizens.'[22] In common with his nineteenth-century predecessors Laski then went on to suggest ways in which bureaucracy could be prevented. Herman Finer likewise continued the earlier practice of comparing the continent of Europe with England and finding bureaucracy in the former only. He insisted that bureaucracy meant government by officials.[23] A distinguished student of the French civil service, W. R. Sharp, determined to call bureaucracy 'the exercise of power by professional administrators' although with that he associated the idea of excessive formalism.[24] In 1937 a Belgian scholar, Daniel Warnotte, reviewed competing concepts of bureaucracy and concluded that the increasing influence of officials was a phenomenon of sufficient sociological importance that the term bureaucracy should be reserved for it alone.[25]

But these definitional exercises were merely holding operations as far as the idea of power of officials was concerned. No attempt was made to develop this concept in the context of research into the other types of power which it implied. However it is also important to point out that even if this concept implied a multiplicity of types of rule, and indeed the proponents were all committed to a type other than bureaucracy, none the less the most influential theory in existence about the power of officials, Michels's 'iron law of oligarchy', denied the reality of this multiplicity. It was precisely this kind of deterministic theory which inhibited the use of a general classificatory scheme of governments in research. The recent development of this concept of bureaucracy has therefore depended on modifying the absoluteness of the Michels's theory. There has had to be a general recognition, firstly, that the issue is not whether officials have power or not, but to what extent they have power; secondly, and consequently, that a typology of government will be based on the *relative* power of different groups and it will be possible for some societies to be more bureaucratic than others.

The work of Arnold Brecht can be cited as an example of the attempt to do justice to the idea of a range of intensity of bureaucratic power. In his essay "How Bureaucracies Develop and Function" (1954), he defines bureaucracy as 'government by officials' and distinguishes two senses of power: the legal right to give orders, and the power to get something done.[26] Officials may possess either type of power, either wholly or partially, and wherever there are officials they will possess some amount of the one or the other type, and Brecht illustrates this thesis to show that there are no countries without bureaucracy. Karl Wittfogel's classic work, *Oriental Despotism* (1957), is the best example of research into the extreme case of bureaucratic power in total form. He develops what he considers to be the suppressed implications of Marx's concept of an Asiatic type of society and argues that the class structure of historical empires such as China was based essentially on the relations of men to the state apparatus. At the heart of this apparatus were the officials.

Credit for the nearest approach to elaborating the full typology of rule which this concept of bureaucracy implies must go to Harold Lasswell and Abraham Kaplan. In *Power and Society* (1950), they outline eight forms of rule, classified according to the class from which the rulers are recruited: bureaucracy ('the form of rule in which the élite is composed of officials'), aristocracy, ethocracy, democracy, virocracy, plutocracy, technocracy and ideocracy.[27] Although the empirical basis of this 'framework for political enquiry' is merely sketched, and it has not been systematically applied, it does suggest the appropriate context for the development of this concept of bureaucracy as rule by officials. A recent attempt to analyse one of those forms of rule (though without reference to Lasswell) is Jean Meynaud's *Technocracy* (1968). It provides some validation of at least part of the Lasswell-Kaplan framework in that Meynaud's examination of power stemming from technical expertise involves him in discussing the power that issues from a predetermined role in an institutional system, i.e. bureaucracy.[28]

We have stressed the use of this concept of bureaucracy as part of an analytical framework for the study of power. At the same time it has been made clear that the linking of this idea of bureaucracy with the theory that all administrative officials acquire power means that any system of public administration can be seen to exemplify bureaucracy. But such a view of public administration may appear distinctly blinkered, for the functions of public administration within society are far more manifold than merely providing members of a governing élite. Therefore public administration has often been referred to as bureaucracy without any special reference to the possession of power being implied. It is to this apparently unimpeachably neutral concept that we now turn.

4/ Bureaucracy as public administration

Paradoxically the most influential proponent of this seemingly neutral concept of bureaucracy was Mussolini. We have seen how well such a concept fitted into the Fascists' programme of absorbing society into the state and how closely related it was to Michels's desire for a neutral concept to play a part in a scientific theory of power. Of course Michels's theory led to viewing bureaucracy as an element of any organizational structure, and we shall examine this line of thought later, but for many the special nature of the state, as seen either by its conservative *laissez-faire* economic opponents or its Fascist supporters, meant reserving the term for public administration.

While right-wing thinkers have found this concept of bureaucracy useful it would be a mistake to infer that those who employ this concept are bound to be right wing. It is an idea to be found widely in the most dispassionate type of political science. But it is interesting that those scholars who have made a particular study of Italy tend to incorporate this idea into their work.[29] Thus Taylor Cole, who discussed Italy's Fascist bureaucracy in the 1930s, introduces his *The Canadian Bureaucracy* (1949), with the following definition: 'The term "bureaucracy" is not used here in an invidious sense . . . but simply refers to a group of human beings or employees who are performing definite functions considered essential by a community.'[30] He proceeds to explain that he does not want to use the term 'civil service' because of its restricted legal sense which prevents it from covering the full range of public employees.

This conceptualization requires two comments. It should first be noted how major emphasis is placed upon the associational aspect of bureaucracy, i.e. on the group performing functions rather than on the functions themselves. With every concept of bureaucracy, as was pointed out in the first chapter, there is an analytical tendency to stress either the group or the activity, to think primarily in institutional or associational terms.[31] The second comment is that, although the functions this group performs are 'definite', they are left undefined, and, although they are 'considered essential', it is not clear who is doing the considering. If we examine this second point more closely we shall find a partial explanation for the emphasis on bureaucracy as a group of bureaucrats.

There is great diversity in the kinds of activities which are undertaken by public employees in any one society and there are large differences between societies as to the functions the state assumes. No theory of public administration can account for the fact that school teachers are civil servants in one country and not another. If public administration is considered to comprise the tasks which public employees have, then the conceptual focus is not provided by the nature of the tasks but by the fact that a number of individuals share a characteristic which gives them a common interest, i.e. employment by the state. For comparative purposes this is the most obvious constant feature.

Even if we attempt to abstract from the general activities of state employees an area we call 'pure' administration we find no structural feature to distinguish civil services from organizations in general, a point which our next concept of bureaucracy accommodates. If there is a crucial differentiating characteristic of civil services it is their use of a vague criterion in decision making known as 'the public interest'. The difficulties in operating this criterion are notorious. Its definition is a matter of political conflict, and therefore theoretically out of the hands of civil servants, but any definition is so dependent on interpretation that there can be no unambiguous central determination of its nature. It is interpreted as it is implemented, and that process is in the hands of civil servants: which brings us back to considering the values and attitudes of the bureaucrats as a group.

The identification of bureaucracy with public administration has, in recent years, usually been a component in the attempt to make the latter a unit of analysis in broad comparative studies or in a general system approach to political life. The result has been to concentrate far more on bureaucracy as a pressure group and a formative influence on societal values than upon processes of administration. These processes may be summed up in terms as content-less as 'A civil service is engaged in meeting the systemic goals of society as a whole', or 'Bureaucratic apparatus is one of the institutions through which goal gratification activity is performed'.[32] The nature of the activities is elusive, but the group is clearly visible.

There are many well-known comparative studies of bureaucracy in this sense. Morstein Marx's *The Administrative State* (1957), proposes a classification of bureaucracies into four types: the Guardian bureaucracy, as in traditional China or Prussia; the Caste bureaucracy, dependent on recruitment from one class only; the Patronage bureaucracy, as in nineteenth-century England or under the Jacksonian system in the United States; and the Merit bureaucracy, tending to be middle class and characterizing modern Western societies.[33] But Morstein Marx also considers other concepts of bureaucracy and makes use of them for analysing other aspects of public administration.

S. N. Eisenstadt's *The Political Systems of Empires* (1963), does not offer a formal definition but normally treats bureaucracy as the body of administrative officials and, after the ruling élite, 'the first group participating in the political struggle'.[34] This study of twenty-seven historical empires outlines a classification of bureaucracies according to their involvement in the political process. They might be (1) service-oriented to rulers and major social strata; (2) totally subservient to the ruler; (3) autonomous and oriented to its own advantage; (4) self-oriented but also serving the polity in general rather than any specific strata.

This concept has been put to considerable use in recent studies of developing societies. It is common to most of the essays in La Palombara's collection, *Bureaucracy and Political Development* (1963). J. T. Dorsey, in his essay on Vietnam, typically defines bureaucracy as 'the "public" or civil governmental administrative components of political systems'.[35] La Palombara concedes the vagueness of this concept of bureaucracy when he introduces the volume. On occasions he says it must be seen as encompassing all public servants, but at other times only those at a high level. In consequence it is 'an accordion-like conceptualization'.[36] It is in the work of another contributor to this volume, Fred W. Riggs, that we find this concept most fully developed, and, in consequence, its particular problems most fully exposed.

In his paper "Agraria and Industria—Toward a Typology of Comparative Administration" (1957), Riggs takes on the task of devising a conceptual framework which would be capable of analysing public administration in societies as diverse as traditional China and contemporary United States.[37] He finds that the idea of administration as the implementation of policies laid down by a legislature is too limited to industrial societies and suggests a definition of 'public administrative system' as 'structures for allocating goods and services in a government'.[38] He finds that his concept of bureaucracy overlaps this, although not completely, and views it as a collective term 'to refer to those whose major occupation or profession is governmental work and who are recruited for this work through means which are neither hereditary nor elective'.[39] Such a concept allows him to do justice to the varying degrees of power bureaucracies may have, and also leaves room for other categories of persons to be involved in the tasks of administration.

But these distinctions become difficult to maintain in the course of analysis. The connections between agrarian bureaucracies and aristocracies are close enough for recruitment to the former to be often *de facto* hereditary. The fact of office-holding remains even if the form of recruitment is not specified. But to think of Riggs' bureaucrats simply as office-holders is still too specific since the notion of an office with a defined authority is more appropriate to the narrow conception of administration he rejects. Perhaps for these reasons Riggs reverts to seeing administration in more traditional terms as 'the process by which policies are implemented' in his 1964 publication, *Administration in Developing Countries*.[40] Here bureaucrats seem simply to be government officials and this is the concept he acknowledges in his contribution to the La Palombara collection.[41]

The 'accordion-like' nature of this concept must be recognized although it is not by any means alone among social science concepts in having this characteristic. In this case the problems arise because of the indefiniteness of the concept of public administration and the immense difficulties there are in adapting it for comparative analysis. Here the idea of bureaucracy, by directing attention to an active political group, may be seen as clarifying issues. Thus Almond and Coleman see the bureaucracy as one interest group among many in *The Politics of Developing Areas* (1960). But then the theoretical content of the concept becomes so thin that it can easily be absorbed into such a general category as 'politicians'. A well-known exponent of systems analysis of politics, David Easton, has a category, the 'authorities', into which government officials fit without special mention.[42] But if there is no wish to focus attention on the political pressure group but rather to find a concept which will highlight the activity involved in public administration, then one must turn to the idea of bureaucracy developed as part of a theory of administration in any organization.

5/ Bureaucracy as administration by officials

We have seen how Max Weber's general concept of bureaucracy (as distinct from the ideal type) simply amounted to administration by appointed officials. But this concept was linked with an explicit framework for organizational analysis in which organizations were seen as tripartite structures in which administrative staffs exercising day to day authority were the central part. Where these staffs were made up of appointees one could talk of bureaucracies. It is fair to see this concept of a specialized function within organizations known as administration as being at the heart of Weber's theory of bureaucracy. Since his time this concept has been maintained particularly strongly by those who have made close study of Weber. Argument among them has centred on whether modern administrative systems have general features in addition to being staffed by appointed officials and whether the ideal type characteristics are the best summary of modern administration.

This concept is especially prevalent in European writing, and this must be attributed to the nature of Continental administration as much as to the influence of Weber. Karl Renner points out in *Demokratie und Bureaukratie* (1947), how concerned the European is with the ideas of office and hierarchy.[43] He argues that all organizations have a bureaucratic apparatus and it is an important fact that the separateness of this apparatus of officials has been reinforced by long-established methods of allocating prestige in European systems of social stratification. H. P. Bahrdt's *Industriebürokratie* (1958), is an excellent example of the use of this concept in a non-government context.[44] He examines the growth of bureaucracy in industry and asks how far automation of office routines will alter concepts of administrative organization. H. Sultan's essay "Bürokratie und Politische Machtbildung" (1955), looks at this concept against a broad background of organizations and considers that the growth of bureaucracy is simply a function of the size of an organization.[45]

American scholars writing in the European tradition on this subject also find this a congenial concept. It is employed by Reinhard Bendix in *Work and Authority in Industry* (1956), although he prefers to speak of the growth of the administrative sector as bureaucratization. We have mentioned how Peter Blau has reverted to this concept after his earlier adherence to the idea of rational organization.[46] The British historian G. E. Aylmer reviews different concepts of bureaucracy to find one suitable for his study of the civil service of Charles I, *The King's Servants* (1961), and decides that historians will find it most useful 'to think of bureaucracy as referring to certain methods of administration'.[47] As examples of these methods he mentions professionalism, regular hierarchy, division into departments and heavy reliance on written records. In this sense, he says, England can be said to have had a bureaucracy since the twelfth century.

The American political scientist, Wallace Sayre, compiled a similar list of characteristics of the administration of any large complex organization: specialization of tasks, hierarchy of authority, body of rules, system of records and personnel with specialized skills and roles.[48] Such a list is not dissimilar to Weber's, but it is crucial that no comment is made as to any level of rationality. Yet it would be wrong to suppose that the universality of these features is non-controversial. We have already mentioned A. L. Stinchcombe's suggestion that the building industry provides a good example of non-centralized administration where control is exercised by independent professional bodies.[49]

Carl Friedrich's efforts to establish the common features of modern administrative systems were also mentioned in the context of discussing his criticisms of Weber.[50] The conceptual strategy he advocates as an alternative to Weber's ideal type method—the systematic comparison of those phenomena known as bureaucracies—has become extremely influential. But if we consider that strategy and Friedrich's general thinking about bureaucracy we will find that it tends to veer away from considering features of administration and towards a more comprehensive concept of organization. In 1932, in collaboration with T. Cole, he wrote *Responsible Bureaucracy—A study of the Swiss Civil Service*. He makes the point there that bureaucracy is to be found as much outside as inside government. As we have already implied, such a perception is a necessary precondition for developing a concept appropriate for all kinds of administration. But he makes the further point that administration and policy are normally too sharply distinguished and it is quite usual to find agencies which combine these functions. So the structural and behavioural elements which for Friedrich make up bureaucracy are found in a wide variety of organizations, and they comprise more than mere administration. But if centralization, differentiation of functions or qualification for office can characterize policy-making agencies as well as administration, can they not also be features of that which is administered? Then it is the organization as a whole which is the subject of analysis. The concept of bureaucracy is on the verge of being recast once again.

6/ Bureaucracy as the organization

Weber's trichotomous view of organizations corresponded well with the hierarchic images of society of his own time. Yet he was prepared to admit, even to emphasize, that the administrator gained power to determine policy. At the same time his idea of the priest and officer being transformed into bureaucrats, while illuminating, stopped short of viewing administrative functions as diffused throughout an organizational hierarchy. For Weber administration meant the exercise of authority. There had to be some who only received and never gave orders. Yet the mode of organizing the administrative staff which he called the ideal type of bureaucracy involved no principles which could not be applied in the structuring of the whole membership of an organization. The requirements of professional qualification, full-time commitment, strict separation of the individual's resources from those of his job, contractual employment, etc., can be attached to any organizational position. If these principles were applied generally and at the same time the fact of diffuse distribution of authority throughout an organization was recognized, it would not be inappropriate to speak of the whole structure as a bureaucracy. From being a sub-system bureaucracy would become the system in its entirety.

It is not possible to impute this line of argument directly and wholly to any one author. But it does briefly indicate how it has happened that Weber has been taken as a starting point, only for the position to be reached that organization and bureaucracy are regarded as synonymous. The very fact of change in organizational structure since his time has meant the adaptation and extension of his terminology. We shall return to this issue in the concluding chapter but for the moment we may note an important indicator of changing social reality: in popular parlance it is common now to talk of any large organization as a bureaucracy. While it would be difficult to confirm this with any degree of certainty, it is likely that this kind of statement: 'The college, from the standpoint of social analysis, is simply one bureaucracy among many others', would have sounded quite foreign to nineteenth-century ears,[51] whereas it no longer seems strange to speak of schools, armies, churches and hospitals as bureaucracies.

In general, therefore, those modern social scientists who write of organizations as bureaucracies do not rely on a complex modification of Weber's theory to justify their concept. They can use everyday language as their authority. Talcott Parsons, introducing his collection of essays, *Structure and Process in Modern Societies* (1960), says: 'One of the most salient structural characteristics of such a society is the prominence in it of relatively large-scale organisations with specialised functions, what rather loosely tend to be called "bureaucracies" '.[52] Others are less guarded about the propriety of this usage. We may cite Hyneman: 'bureaucracy as an abstraction is big organisation, and any big organisation is specifically a bureaucracy'; Simon that bureaucracy is 'an approximate synonym for large scale organisation'; Presthus, 'the terms "big organisation" and "bureaucratic structures" are synonymous'; and Etzioni, 'There are many synonyms for the term, *organisation*. One, *bureaucracy*, has two disadvantages.'[53]

The disadvantages Etzioni has in mind are the popular negative connotations and the possible assumption by those familiar with Max Weber's work that the organization would be ordered along the lines of the ideal type. This second possibility has concerned others too. Just as Friedrich advocates the comparative study of systems of administration, so those who have identified bureaucracy with the organization as a whole have supported research to establish what dimensions do characterize organizations. Of course such a programme is itself dependent on the concept of organization which is held at the outset of research. Some think of organizations only as social units oriented to specific goals. Others implicitly or explicitly have a wide concept of organization and limit their field of research to complex, or large-scale, or formal, or modern organizations. Then, as Ferrel Heady writes, 'bureaucracy is a form of organization. Organizations either are bureaucracies or they are not, depending on whether or not they have these characteristics.' [54]

There are almost as many listings of the characteristics making up bureaucracy as there are authors who hold this concept. Presthus lists size, specialization, hierarchy, status authority, oligarchy, co-optation, rationality and 'efficiency'; Bennis mentions a chain of command, rules, division of labour, selection on ground of individual competence and impersonality; Heady reduces the list to three items for which he claims there is 'substantial' agreement: hierarchy, differentiation or specialization, and qualification or competence. [55] The fact that Heady introduces the notion of 'substantial agreement' between authors suggests another conceptual strategy which is becoming fashionable among the proponents of this concept. With the proliferation of different lists of characteristics it is now possible to undertake an 'empirical' research project to determine what is common to the lists. A new depiction of bureaucracy results, which includes those characteristics on which there is general agreement. [56] But the search for such a consensus may result in such a diversity of items being revealed that in the end doubt is cast upon the usefulness of the concept of bureaucracy. [57] It may appear as more of an impediment than an aid to agreed conceptual framework for the comparative study of organizations.

Bureaucracy as organization is also a difficult idea. The facts of organizational structure are not unambiguous data, to be recorded by anyone who might care to observe, but abstract and elusive phenomena which depend on interpretative inventiveness. In particular, the boundaries of organizations are difficult to draw. Just as it proved complicated to draw a line between administration and organization, so it is hard to see where organization ends and society begins. Hierarchy, rules, division of labour, careers, qualifications seem to pervade modern society, and are not simply housed in separate organizations. Perhaps we can speak of organizations as being bureaucratic only because they are a part of a wider bureaucracy—modern society itself.

7/ Bureaucracy as modern society

We cannot be surprised by what may be called the apotheosis of bureaucracy, its acceptance into that pantheon of ideas which attempt to capture the essence of a society and among which are such concepts as democracy, communism, capitalism and socialism. It may be seen as a development inherent in an idea which in its conception was set on the same plane as democracy, aristocracy and monarchy. It is just as appropriate to employ 'democratic' as an epithet for a society as for a government. But if this development has always been a potentiality, we should not underestimate the arduousness of the gestation period.

The tradition of Western thought about societal types was largely captured by Marx and his followers. We have already explained why the concept of bureaucracy could not occupy a dominant place in Marxist thought. The idea of a bureaucratic society could only be developed by Marxist heretics. Rizzi and Djilas provide examples. Among the opponents of Marxism the most notable approximation to the idea of society as bureaucracy is in Mosca's work. Since Mosca, the most widely known Western expression of the view that society is dominated by bureaucrats is that made in James Burnham in 1941: *The Managerial Revolution* (significantly enough, the author was formerly a Marxist). While stressing the importance of the managerial group in the economy, Burnham argues in that book that there is no sharp separation between them and political officials. 'To say that the ruling class is the managers is almost the same thing as to say that it is the state bureaucracy.'[53]

However, even if Burnham envisages the fusion of state and private management, it is none the less true that his theory, like that of Marx or of Mosca, considers a society's type to be stamped on it by the character of its ruling class. Mosca and Burnham are talking of bureaucratic societies largely in the sense of societies ruled by bureaucracies rather than societies which have become bureaucracies. The difference between the two concepts is wide. Karl Wittfogel, for instance, speaks of bureaucratic society where an undifferentiated peasantry making up perhaps 95 per cent of the population supports the ruling bureaucratic class. The societies which Djilas analyses have highly differentiated proletariats in which every member has a specified organizational role; the whole structure may be seen as bureaucracy.

The ideological desire for the fusion of state and society became most concrete in Italian Fascism. But commentators on Fascist Italy have seen the corporate state as a framework fitted over an order which was well adapted to it.[59] Karl Mannheim has argued that changes in social structure in the twentieth century have in any case made the opposition of the concepts of state and society out of date. 'This dualism usually equates "state" with "bureaucracy" and society with the conglomeration of vigorous organisations that successfully claim the epithets "free and private" '.[60] He finds that this dualism is obsolete for several reasons. In respect of power, methods of recruitment, public significance and the personality types of members, he sees no difference between private and public organizations. Their spheres overlap so that 'public responsibility is interwoven in the whole fabric of society'.[61]

A similar conclusion has been reached by those who have begun their analysis at the other end and considered the internal structure of organizations. As we have shown in the context of argument with Weber it has become normal to stress that the framework of organizational regulations reflects wider social structure. Even those areas of social life which seem to be interstitial, and outside the sole control of any one organization, exhibit codes of rules which may have emerged out of a common interest in formalizing relations, for example in areas as different as business and sport. We can see Crozier's emphasis on the bureaucratic culture of France as a culmination of this way of thinking.[62] As R. V. Presthus has expressed this in *The Organizational Society* (1962), 'organizations are indeed miniatures of society'. Since he regards 'big organizations' and 'bureaucratic structures' as synonymous we can conclude that it is not incongruous to think of bureaucracy as a type of society.[63]

It is interesting to see how this culminating point has also been implied in the use of the idea of bureaucratization. Very often this term has been used simply to connote the growth of bureaucracy. Therefore it may take on as many meanings as bureaucracy itself. But it is a verbal substantive. It implies a unit, be it group or society, which is being bureaucratized. In the 1920s it was quite normal to speak of the bureaucratization of the firm, meaning the introduction of systematic administration and the growth of the number of purely administrative employees.[64] But the impact of this process is not limited to the firm. Its employees are also members of society and take to it their organizational experience. As the firm grows its influence as a unit increases. If the firm itself is viewed as a bureaucracy then we can conceive of the bureaucratization of society in terms of an increase in the number and size of its organizations. But we can also see bureaucratization as the subjection of society to the influence of the attitudes and values of bureaucrats, or, in Arnold Gehlen's words, 'the development of an immanent perfectionism'.[65]

S. N. Eisenstadt draws a distinction between the growth of bureaucracy and bureaucratization which he defines as the 'excessive domination by the bureaucracy of parts of its environment'.[66] But the ever expanding nature of the concept of bureaucracy means that in practice this distinction must break down. For the growth of bureaucracies (administrations or organizations) proceeds by the continual incorporation of new elements into the bureaucracy, so that they become constituent parts of it.[67] The growth of organizations involves the bureaucratization of society, and that is tantamount to society becoming bureaucracy.

What we have outlined here is complex. It requires further interpretation and we shall return to that task. But, before that, it is worth taking a brief look at the various remedies which have been prescribed for bureaucracy. Those who advocate alternatives, by implication specify all the more clearly the nature of the condition they seek to remedy.

6/Bureaucracy and the Theorists of Democracy

The changing intellectual context

The idea of bureaucracy arose out of a concern for the proper place of the official in modern government. We have seen, in particular, how the nineteenth-century writers contrasted bureaucracy with democracy. They discerned numerous ways in which the use and usages of public officials subverted democratic values. In other words, the phenomena which were held to constitute bureaucracy were defined as significant topics for analysis by their relation to the values of democracy, and, because of their conflict with those values, were held to be problems requiring solution. Similarly, the remedies which were suggested for bureaucracy were designed to realize the very values which defined the nature of the disease. It follows that as the values of democracy were reformulated so the concept of bureaucracy was recast.

When the evaluative elements in the nineteenth-century theory of bureaucracy are exposed so clearly, an easy explanation of the neglect of that literature suggests itself. Much effort has been spent in this century in separating the advocacy of values from the analysis of facts. Our discussions have reflected this. We have analysed ideological literature separately from modern social science. It may well appear that the old argument about the relation of democracy and bureaucracy has been rendered futile by the demonstration that it involves two sets of problems: the specification of the values of democracy, and the gathering of data about the place of public officials in modern government.

Yet the problem of bureaucracy is still raised. Scholars and citizens are still concerned to offer solutions in the light of their conception of true democracy. We can still find conceptualizations of bureaucracy which would have fitted easily into nineteenth-century discussions. For example, Herman Finer, reviewing some of the more indiscriminate accusations of bureaucracy made in the 1940s, considers that charge appropriate only where there is 'administration by bureaus of government officials who are abusing the function for which they were appointed'.[1] The dual character of this concept, both empirical and normative, should be apparent. To demonstrate the existence of bureaucracy it is not sufficient simply to indicate the mode of behaviour of public officials. It must be shown that this behaviour does not correspond with their duty, 'the function for which they were appointed'. But this function is always in dispute. It is the subject of the endless debate about the true nature of democracy.

We are concerned in this chapter with those who still pose 'the problem of bureaucracy' and suggest solutions to it. So long as there are types of public officials and sets of values which are held to be an inherent part of 'real' democracy this 'problem of bureaucracy' will continue to be raised. Moreover, it would be quite mistaken to suppose that modern advances in social and political science have rendered the old problem settings redundant and no longer important. On the contrary, discussion has been raised to new levels of sophistication and of importance. We should recall that Max Weber was one of the major advocates of the clear separation of factual statements from evaluative judgements. Yet he did not retreat from suggesting answers to the problem of the relationship of bureaucracy to democracy. He analysed this issue with characteristic dispassion. He drew the line so clearly between the two modes of discourse only to mark the point when he was changing from the one to the other.[2]

The writing which followed may be seen as occupying a position somewhere between ideology and social science. It is not ideological in the sense of directly advocating certain values. Rather it seeks to analyse values for their meaning and implications. Indeed the personal commitment of the analyst to those values is not required. It is not 'social scientific' in the sense of having as a prime purpose the accumulation of propositions of a general and explanatory nature about how institutions operate. Instead, it sifts the propositions of social science to discover information which is *significant* for certain value positions. But clearly it is a literature which is dependent on the prior separation of fact and value, and many would see it as characteristic of Western political thought. We shall not argue about its proper designation—whether it should be labelled political theory, philosophy or science. It is sufficient, in this context, to call its exponents 'the theorists of democracy'.

It cannot be denied that it is often very difficult to determine what is ideological and what is social scientific, and, since the definition of this intermediate category is dependent on such a distinction, we must be prepared to find ambiguously located writing. We have already discovered that much of what is written around the concepts of bureaucracy as rational or inefficient administration involves the application of evaluative criteria and the specification of the nature of those values. It was the intention rather than the achievement of those writers which warranted discussing those concepts in the previous chapter and not in this. Similarly we can turn to East European discussions of the way to realize popular sovereignty through local self-government and find that this belongs properly to the literature of the theorists of democracy.[3] Certainly we shall have to consider, after discussing their work, whether the democratic theorists do not, after all, allow an unexamined ideology to colour their reasoning.

If the above analysis is correct the concept of bureaucracy we are discussing here cannot be equated with any of the concepts of the previous chapter, although any of those may at one time or another be considered as an aspect of the threat to democracy. Even the concept of bureaucracy as rule by officials, while closest to nineteenth-century preoccupations, has been incorporated into neutral typologies of government and is regarded as permitting argument as to whether it is or is not compatible with the idea of democracy.[4] It must be made quite clear at the outset of this discussion that the concept under scrutiny is of public officials defeating the objects of democracy. It differs, therefore, from the concepts considered in the previous chapter in its high evaluative content and the consequent relativity of its application to empirical phenomena. Whether the operations of public officials are to be judged as bureaucracy depends on how the values of democracy are construed and which of them are held to be offended. For each interpretation of democracy there is a corresponding idea of bureaucracy.

At this point a tiresome, but unavoidable, terminological issue must be raised. Not every writer on the theme of the threat to democracy from officialdom calls that threat 'bureaucracy'. Many do, but the majority reserve the term for one or other of the concepts discussed in the previous chapter. Sometimes this difference in usage may be symptomatic of deeper disagreements. Friedrich's use of the term for administration by officials signifies his belief that it is not the power of officials which presents a problem, but the way in which that power is used. Herman Finer's reservation of 'bureaucracy' for the situation where officials threaten democracy expresses his disagreement with that position. But both Friedrich and Finer are concerned with the problem of the compatibility of the practices of modern public administration with the values of democracy. In the ensuing pages we shall call this 'the problem of bureaucracy'. This phrase is conveniently ambiguous as far as terminology is concerned. It does not make clear whether the problem is *called* bureaucracy, as with Finer, or is *posed by* bureaucracy, as with Friedrich. What concerns us primarily is not the varying terminology, but the identity of the concept.

We may view the increasing sophistication of argument about the problem of bureaucracy by the theorists of democracy simply as a facet of intellectual development, the result of the refinement of philosophical analysis and the accumulation of scientific evidence. But it can also be seen as a response to new factors in the social environment. Put at its simplest level, the application of the idea of democracy to a city state and to an industrialized society with a population of 50 million is bound to give different results. Hence, while we can point to certain basic principles which would be held to inhere in democracy in both the eighteenth and twentieth centuries—that government must express the will of the governed, that popularly elected representatives should have a major share of government, that the rule of law must regulate governmental procedure, that the governed should be informed of the decisions taken on their behalf—the very fact of the growth of huge cadres of public officials raises problem to which those principles give no direct answers.

The bulk of constitutional theory in the nineteenth century was devoted to elaborating the division of functions between legislative, executive and judicial organs of the democratic state. Minimal attention was given to specifying the place of the public official in this scheme. His purely instrumental position was largely assumed. But as administration has loomed larger and larger, to become regarded as the core of modern government, the criterion of instrumentality has increasingly been seen as an inadequate means for specifying the nature of democratic administration. Different criteria, such as accountability, responsibility, responsiveness, or representativeness, are held to be the appropriate standards implied by the values of democracy, to which public services must be kept if they are not to become bureaucracies. We shall see how each of these criteria is used in attempts both to diagnose and to cure the problem of bureaucracy, and we shall see that each involves a different interpretation of what is most basic to the concept of democracy.

The diagnosis of bureaucracy

We may distinguish three basic positions as to the functions of public officials in the democratic state. The first is that officials have acquired too much power and need to be brought back to their proper functions. The second is that officials necessarily have ever growing power and the task is to see that this is exercised wisely. The third is that power necessarily accrues to officials and the quest should be for methods whereby their services might be dispensed with altogether.

Of these positions, the third is clearly the most radical but also the least clearly articulated; the second the most orthodox, and the first is nearest to the concerns of the nineteenth century. It has been most popular with lawyers, for reasons which will rapidly be apparent. The threat to democracy is not seen as arising from the incompetence of public officials, but almost from their excessive reliability and diligence. The most celebrated exposition of this theme is that of Lord Chief Justice Hewart in *The New Despotism* (1929). The root of the problem he sees as the increasing amount of delegated legislation and power to adjudicate which belongs to the modern civil service. Statutes are passed which allow details to be filled in subsequently by officials, provision is made for departmental regulations to have the force of law, decisions are made against which the citizen has no recourse at law. He sees such practices emerging from an ethos which regards the permanent official as the expert and representative government as a hindrance to efficient transaction of public business.

Hewart's book caused sufficient alarm in Britain for a Committee on Ministers' Powers to be set up. Its report in 1932 concluded that delegated legislation was an inevitable feature of modern government. It allowed Parliament to concentrate on basic principles and ensured that these were operated with flexibility.[5] In the United States an equivalent to Hewart's treatise is J. M. Beck's *Our Wonderland of Bureaucracy* (1932), which bears the sub-title, 'A study of the growth of bureaucracy in the federal government and its destructive effect upon the constitution'. Beck, a former solicitor general, draws on Hewart but extends his analysis to a broader political front and attacks the growth of a socialistic state. He takes his stand on what he calls the great objectives of the Constitutional Convention and especially on article 1, section 8 of the Constitution which provides for taxes to be collected 'for the general welfare of the United States'. He argues that this phrase was meant to impose limits on government but that it has been construed so as to give almost unlimited powers.[6] Under the protection of this article, the administration drafts extensive legislation, and puts itself in the position of prosecutor, jury and judge.

This theme has been taken up repeatedly since the 1930s and has been particularly popular with opponents of socialism.[7] Among professional students of government, however, it has taken a modified form. The tendency is to argue that delegated legislation is here to stay. The problem is that it has tended to outstrip the standard methods of direction and control which have been used in the past. Writers such as Herman Finer and C. S. Hyneman do not disregard the danger to democracy in the modern development of public administration, but they tend to see it as potential rather than actual. The appropriate criterion against which to measure democratic public administration is the responsibility of officials, in the sense of arrangements existing which ensure that their actions will be scrutinized, corrected or punished as need be.[8] Where such arrangements break down the problem of bureaucracy arises.

When we turn to the second of the positions on the functions of the public officials which we have distinguished, we find that Finer's and Hyneman's views are one side of an important argument in the modern study of government. While they agree that the official is more involved than ever in complex policy-forming tasks, their emphasis is on the formal limits within which this task may be executed. C. J. Friedrich's name is particularly associated with the view that the formal delimitation of the scope of official activity is less important for democracy than the type of advice which the official gives and the spirit in which he interprets his tasks. The policy-making role of the official is not something to be grudgingly conceded, but is a vital aspect of his tasks. He sees the distinction of policy making and execution as overdrawn.[9] Some of those who follow this line of argument extend it to the point of offering a redefinition of public administration to include policy formulation.[10]

This different emphasis on the functions of public officials involves a different interpretation of what is to be understood by democratic administration and hence a different perspective on the problem of bureaucracy. Finer's elucidation of the criterion of responsibility to mean accountability is replaced by a concern for the responsiveness of the official to public needs. Another way of expressing this contrast is through considering the differing emphasis on the concept of democracy which it involves. Those who consider the functions of the official in danger of being over-extended are concerned primarily with the ideas of the rule of law and governmental control by elected representatives. Those who believe that the policy-making functions of officials are insufficiently appreciated are more intent on developing the ideas of government expressing a basic popular will and of a free flow of information between governors and governed.[11]

From this standpoint the problem of bureaucracy arises when officials fail to understand or respond to public needs. The occasions on which this may happen vary, and, indeed, it may occur even when formal control procedures are tightly drawn. On this interpretation the German civil service was not responding to public needs and was acting irresponsibly in co-operating with Hitler, even though they were fulfilling their legal obligations. At another extreme, public officials who fail to obtain necessary professional expertise and fail to make use of specialized knowledge are also non-responsive. In the formulation and interpretation of policy the official is expected to make use of the best sources of information and maintain contact with all levels of the public.[12]

This last requirement leads to an elaboration of the criterion of responsiveness in the direction of representativeness. It has been argued that the free flow of information between officials and public is dependent on a shared culture, on a set of mutual understandings which can only be achieved if in fact officials are drawn from all segments of a community. Responsiveness is made to depend on the scope of recruitment procedures. J. D. Kingsley advances this view in his study of the British civil service, *Representative Bureaucracy* (1944). He argues that the civil servant is a 'permanent politician' upon whose views the policy of a modern government is greatly reliant.[13] But the process of recruitment produces a service with a narrow class background, adapted to working with Conservative Party politicians but likely to be in conflict with a Labour Party government. In the event, Labour Party politicians have gone out of their way to stress the dedication of their officials, but the limitations of social background are often mentioned as an aspect of the problem of bureaucracy in other contexts.[14] Thus G. Sjöberg argues that public administration is insensitive to the lower class and that since that class cannot understand public administration there is bound to be conflict between that class and officials. He records how the Negro leadership has attacked the U.S. Department of Labor for its assumption that it is the Negro lower-class family which requires restructuring rather than the administrative system.[15]

This emphasis on the group characteristics of civil services can lead to the third point of view concerning the functions of public officials which was mentioned at the beginning of this section. On this view the very existence of a body of public officials, defined as separate from the general population even if drawn representatively from it, with its own professional standards, must lead to the formation of sectional interests. An identity of values between officials and the public cannot be expected and the problem of bureaucracy is inherent in the situation. This radical position, which owes much to Marx and sociological analyses of bureaucracy, sees the conflict between democracy and public administration as inevitable in differentiated societies with distinct administrative staffs. Only the form of the conflict alters. It may take extreme forms, such as interference by civil servants in elections or strike action calculated to subvert the state. It may be expressed more mildly, such as by alliance with sectional interests, resistance to outside inspection, or simply activity as any other political pressure group.[16]

At its most basic the dilemma which is posed is this: no special group in society can reflect the interests of all because it has interests of its own. This sectional interest will always be expressed in policy making while the various interests of other groups will be variably realized. Any public policy decision will be a political one into which the sectional interest will be intimately bound. F. E. Rourke has examined the problems of secrecy and publicity as special cases of this dilemma. Secrecy in public administration, recognized by Weber as a source of bureaucratic power, has been less prevalent in the United States than in Europe. But its opposite, publicity, can equally well serve as a means of enhancing the power of public agencies. It can be used to raise the level of public support in the community and in special interest groups, and it is impossible to distinguish clearly between the contribution to the public interest and the ambitions of the agency.[17]

No easy remedy seems to offer itself for this third construction of the problem of bureaucracy, but before considering this issue we must return to the two earlier positions.

The remedies for bureaucracy

As the concept of the problem varies, so do the remedies that are proposed. Those who are concerned by the degree of involvement by officials in policy making and the range of their discretion advocate various kinds of formal control mechanisms. The particular type of control which is favoured varies according to the area of official power which is under scrutiny. The public official can exercise influence on decisions before they are made by giving advice or sifting information. The decision which is made may formally confer wide discretionary powers on those who have to implement it, or such powers may *de facto* come to exist because the decision is open to various interpretations. Furthermore, these opportunities for the official to exercise power exist at all levels of government, from relations with ministers to direct dealings with the public, from foreign policy decisions to an individual's income tax assessment.

Hence the proposals which are made range from greater control by representative bodies to more legal protection for the citizen in the form of administrative law. Hewart would prefer to see the end of discretionary legislation altogether, while others look to the example of France for an elaborated system of law governing the relations of officials and citizens.[18] In Britain the idea of ministerial responsibility and the subjection of ministers to the parliamentary question have been regarded as the main form of popular control, but, in recent years, there has been support for the idea of parliamentary committees to investigate departmental policy on analogy with congressional committees in the United States.[19] A further alternative is the advocation of new formal agencies of control outside the established representative and legal institutions. For example W. W. Boyer proposes an Office of Administrative Procedure to keep administrative action constantly under review.[20]

A Parliamentary Commissioner has been appointed in Britain, on analogy with the Scandinavian *Ombudsman*, to investigate complaints against civil service administration.

The most elaborate exposition of the case for formal control and the variety of forms which it can assume is contained in C. S. Hyneman's *Bureaucracy in a Democracy* (1950). He takes issue with Friedrich and similar theorists by arguing that the key condition for democratic administration is the existence of authoritative ways of instructing officials. The authoritative bodies in the United States are Congress and the president assisted by the central staff agencies and the courts. Hyneman argues that the means of direction and control which are at their disposal are far more numerous and effective, at least potentially, than is usually recognized to be the case. Limits are set in prescribing the tasks of administration which are made more real by specifying the nature of the organization required and the finance available. Control over appointments, review and investigating procedures provide additional tools for the task of ensuring democratic administration. Hyneman's outline of the system of administrative direction and control in the United States expresses fully the spirit of Herman Finer's view that responsibility is ensured through 'an arrangement of correction and punishment'.[21]

The more extreme statements of the case for greater formal control have often come in for severe criticism. E. Pendleton Herring speaks of how 'Lord Hewart looks with a futile nostalgia to the rule of law as interpreted by the courts'.[22] But the more sophisticated exponents of this case are not open to the charge that they fail to see the inevitability of discretion and delegated legislation. In the search for limits on these aspects of the official's power their existence is admitted. However the very emphasis which is involved in this quest for formal limits has been attacked as the wrong approach to the problem of bureaucracy. Herbert Simon has expressed himself strongly and succinctly on this issue in commenting on the 1949 Hoover Commission Report.[23] That report criticizes public administration in the United States for confused lines of authority and consequent impairment of responsibility and accountability, and also for lack of staff services. Simon argues that the existing staff agencies which provide 'independent' reviews of administrative action are themselves largely responsible for lack of clear lines of authority. The establishment of such agencies involves increased operating costs, the development of a new interest group and limits on operating departments which will manifest themselves as red tape.

This criticism can be stated in more general terms. At the simplest, it poses the old question of '*Quis custodiet ipsos custodes?*' At the most complex level, it involves the general theory of the nature and functioning of rules in social life. No rule applies itself. It is applied by men who have the twin tasks of interpreting its meaning and assessing whether the empirical conditions exist to justify its application. In other words, judgement must be exercised, and every rule is dependent on the spirit in which this judgement is made. This leads some to argue that there cannot possibly be 'neutral' administrators. For some the interpretation of a rule will be too literal and reflect a spirit of red tape, for others that same interpretation will appear too loose and exhibit the official's abuse of power.[24] But if this dilemma exists for the official, it exists equally for those who are appointed to control officials. Even if those who control officials are elected representatives, the results of persistent examination of the extent to which officials adhere to rules may very well be self-defeating, generating evasion, defensiveness and only minimally satisfactory performance.

The resemblance of this argument among the democratic theorists to the criticisms which have been levelled at Max Weber is not coincidental. C. J. Friedrich is an important figure in both areas of controversy. In important respects the concept of democratic administration which he advances is designed to be in direct opposition to Max Weber's account of purely rational administration, which is seen to correspond to the authoritarianism and legalism of the German imperial civil service. Yet the remedies for bureaucracy which he advocates also have characteristics which have been imputed to the more powerful continental civil services. In his study of the Swiss civil service he proposes the active participation of civil servants in basic decision making in order to enhance their morale. He suggests 'partial self-government' in the service to inhibit undue public interference.[25] Elsewhere he insists that the responsible administrator is one who is responsible both to public sentiment and to technical knowledge. Neither of these factors can be assured by decree.[26] They depend on the values and calibre of the officials themselves.

It should now be apparent that the differing remedies offered for bureaucracy reflect some of the basic antitheses in social and political science. In this argument there are echoes of the disputes about the relative importance of formal and informal sources of cohesion in organizations, punishment or treatment of criminals, permissiveness or discipline in socialization, or, indeed, of force or consensus as the basis of social order. The opponents of emphasis on formal controls in public administration are maintaining that if it is necessary for the individual to have personal autonomy and freedom of decision, and necessary for society that individuals have an inner commitment to democratic values, then no exceptions can be made from these requirements in the case of public officials and civil services.

The conclusion is that the commitment of the official to democratic values is a more important safeguard for democracy than any formal system of control. Methods of achieving this result include a strong emphasis on professional competence and a recruitment policy which both selects persons of the right calibre and ensures that their social background is such that they have a ready sympathy for all sections of the community.[27] (It hardly needs mention that most social systems make these two aspects of recruitment incompatible.) Professionalism and representativeness are expected to enhance public trust, and the result of this will be a decline in the demand for formal controls. But the beneficent effects do not end here. A decline in formal controls imposed from the outside results in a reduction of formal control within the official hierarchy. The official feels less threatened and trust between officials is enhanced. B. H. Baum has concluded that decentralization depends on mutual trust.[28] But decentralization is associated with speed of decision. This in turn reduces friction with the public and reinforces public trust. The vicious circle of bureaucracy has become benign.

None the less, it is possible to detect a note in this idea of democratic administration which seems dissonant. While the stress is on responsiveness, this is achieved through autonomy. As has often been remarked, professionalism may enhance the listening ability of the official, but it also increases his distance from the source of the noise.[29] It has been pointed out that American officials are more representative of different strata of the population than congressmen are.[30] But they are still highly selected, and in the higher echelons have an educational and professional experience which marks them off from the rest of the population. Recent writers, such as N. E. Long, W. S. Sayre and C. E. Jacob, are in unison in saying that the federal government service makes up a fourth and equal arm of government.[31] P. Woll's remark is typical: 'American bureaucracy takes its place as an equal partner with the President, Congress and the judiciary.'[32] But if it is 'equal' it is involved in a struggle for power with its equals. What relation, then, do the other three arms of government bear to the public to which the public service is so 'responsive'?

There would appear to be more to the criterion of responsiveness than the internalization of democratic values by the official. This is indicated by Friedrich's remark: 'At best responsibility in a democracy will become fragmentary because of the indistinct voice of the principal whose agents the officials are supposed to be—the vast, heterogeneous masses composing the people.'[33] The key terms here are 'indistinct voice' and 'vast, heterogeneous masses'. What is there to respond to? The implications are clearly seen in Herring's *Public Administration and the Public Interest* (1936). Also advocating responsiveness, he says that it is necessary to 'promote a purpose of the state over and above the medley of interests that compose it'.[34] He gives this task to the officials and, thereby, gives as perfect an evocation of Hegel's position as the changed conditions of this century would allow.[35]

What the advocates of responsiveness have to offer may appear strikingly similar to a characterization of bureaucracy which Mill suggested, 'a practice which keeps the citizens in a relation to the government like that of children to their guardians'.[36] The modern public official is revealed as a paternalistic aristocrat. The public speaks, yet it is the official who chooses when to listen, to whom, and with what degree of attention. Mill saw a sharp conflict between bureaucracy and representative democracy. He saw as a clear feature of the latter that it enhanced the capacity for political action and guaranteed the power of organized action being diffused in a community. It is this belief, that it is intrinsic to the idea of democracy that the power of decision is not reserved to the few, which sustains the third position on the problem of bureaucracy which we identified. It is the foundation of the demands for citizen participation, workers' control or student power.[37] It has received no authoritative exposition.

To end this chapter on this note is to recall our discussion of the ideologists. The same theme appears: a hint of an emerging radical discussion of the decision-making structure of the state and the organizations which dominate modern society. The separate treatment of the writers we have discussed in this chapter was justified by their critical posture towards both the facts and values they consider. But it is not unfair to comment that there are sufficient unexamined assumptions behind their arguments to warrant saying that theirs is simply a sophisticated expression of the ideology of Western societies. It is regularly assumed that, while all men are members of interest groups, a small number can see the interests of all. Democracy is held to be about this common interest: it has little to do with the locus of political action. It is taken for granted that the area of state action will continue to grow, that public officials will increase in numbers, that their calibre must always be improved because their decisions are becoming more complex.

For the radical, it is precisely the ready acquiescence of the Western democratic theorists to this conceptual framework which perpetuates the modern problem of bureaucracy.

Conclusion:
The Concept
of Bureaucracy in Social
and Political Science

It has often been held against social scientists that they invent unnecessary new terminology to conceal a poverty of ideas. This may, on occasion, be a justified charge. But this study would seem to suggest a different failing. We have identified many different concepts being presented in the same verbal dress. The name 'bureaucracy' has been applied to government by officials, public administration, the administration of any organization, administrative efficiency or inefficiency, and the modern organization, to mention only some of the many concepts discussed. This appears to evidence not an excess, but a poverty of terminological inventiveness. Some explanation is necessary.

In the first place we should recall that each twist in the meaning of bureaucracy has had close affiliations with what went before. This book will have failed if it has not succeeded in showing the steps whereby 'bureaucracy' came to be applied to a ruling group of officials after it had referred to a method of government by officials; how it came to denote any rational administration after it had referred to the system of modern administration; or how it came to be used for any modern organization after being applied merely to the administrative sub-system. Each step of this kind has proved intelligible. It is the end-product, a bevy of competing concepts, which is bewildering. Few concepts in social science have undergone such a continual process of fragmentation and transformation. It is this which means that we are faced with much more than the usual problem of discovering minor verbal disagreements and shifts of emphasis in the differing formulations of a concept.

For the first part of a tentative explanation of this process let us consider some of the well-attested facts about the very areas to which concepts of bureaucracy have been applied. There are many accounts of the growth of state power in the eighteenth century, of the way government took on more and more functions in the nineteenth, and of the way this growth has been prolonged in the twentieth.[1] An obvious indicator of this development is the growth in the percentage of the population who are employed in public services which has taken place in almost every decade in every society.[2] Similarly many sources tell us how organizations have increased in number and size in modern society, and how, with this growth, there has been an increase in the proportion of employees who are engaged in administrative tasks.[3]

These quantitative changes have been accompanied by qualitative changes in organizational structure, both in the case of government and other organizations. A change which begins early in industrialized societies is the separation of domicile from place of work. This is accompanied by a separation of those who produce from those who own the product. These changes occupied the attention of the nineteenth century. This century has been concerned with a further separation: that between those who own and those who control the process of production. These 'separations' are usually expressed in terms particularly applicable to industry, but they are equally appropriate to other sectors. For example, we can replace the terms 'manager' and 'owner' by 'civil servant' and 'politician', and discern the same process at work.

Society now includes a distinct and recognizable group of managers and administrators with similar job experiences, interests and values. Their career structures, salaries and the qualifications demanded of them are all special aspects of a wide range of administrative techniques which are employed in both public and private organizations. Ideologies of 'good administration' help to stereotype practices in all sectors and have an impact on the values of the wider society. Finally, it is no longer possible for the citzen to remain aloof from these changes. He necessarily comes into contact with organizations in a wide range of everyday activities. That contact is routinized and recorded to become both an element of organizational structure and a basic factor in the individual's experience and outlook.

These phenomena are central to our understanding of the specific features of contemporary society. We may find isolated historical anticipations, but fundamentally they are novel, and certainly they are new in the perception of the men who have observed and commented on them. Some facet of them has always been the focus of attention for the writers we have been examining, and it is within this broad context that ideas of bureaucracy have developed. The term 'bureaucracy' was first used for novel features of government, but as these were replaced in novelty by the successive changes we have mentioned, the term was applied to the emergent features, taking on new meanings even while the old usages were still current. As a neologism, applied to a rapidly developing sector of modern society, the conditions for a stabilization of its usage simply did not exist. With each major structural change there arose a new concept of bureaucracy.

It is possible to illustrate how this proliferation of concepts is coupled with a preservation of terminology. Let us consider the concept of bureaucracy as government by officials. It may be broadly conceived, and held to comprise a range of features such as a hierarchic chain of offices, specific appointment procedures, emphasis on written regulations, set administrative routines, discretionary powers for officials and their exercise of state coercion. The relative emphasis given to the various features of the concept may not be explicitly stated, and may vary with personal interpretation.

Now let us consider what happens to this concept when organizations develop which have many of these characteristics: hierarchy, appointing procedures, etc. They may differ from what has hitherto been called bureaucracy in one respect only—the exercise of state coercion. But, although this was never explicit, many users of this concept may have regarded the aspect of coercion as unimportant. The similarity between governmental and non-governmental organization in respect of the other features may be so great that, for these people, there will appear to be no reason for withholding the designation 'bureaucracy' from the latter while giving it to the former.

But this conceptual development will not satisfy those who regard the use of state coercion by officials as an intrinsic part of the idea of bureaucracy. The designation of non-governmental organizations as bureaucracies incites them to make explicit their own emphasis on the importance of state coercion. They now prefer to regard as contingent the other features of bureaucracy which occasioned the extension of the concept to non-governmental organizations. The result is two competing concepts of bureaucracy, one referring to the structure of organizations generally, the other to governments where officials exercise state power. At the same time the original concept will still have its adherents.

If this account is a fair paradigm of the processes of thought examined in the preceding chapters, we may identify two basic ingredients in the development of ideas on bureaucracy. The first is a broad concept with vague outline. A new identifying label such as 'bureaucracy' will be symptomatic of the lack of time which has elàpsed for agreement to emerge on the concept's scope (although this is true only where there is no authoritative invention and definition of the term). The second ingredient is that the situation which is being conceptualized should itself be changing and evolving into qualitatively quite different forms.

This combination of social and ideal factors may be held to provide a reasonably satisfying explanation of the process we may call 'terminological conservation and conceptual change'. We could speculate further and argue that social change is itself so disturbing that it is necessary to the individual that at least the illusion of security is provided by the conservation of terminology. But it would be idle to speculate on the psychological functions of this process. What we can see is that there is no inherent reason for the process to come to a halt. Only a general consciousness of the factors involved in conceptual development and a determination to seek ways of improving the precision of our thinking about society can'assist. It is to be hoped that this book may play some small part in this, and that the reader may now be able to pick his way more easily through the conceptual thickets which the term 'bureaucracy' conceals.

But enhanced consciousness, though an aid, does not of itself solve the immediate problem of the working social scientist. He writes about men who speak of bureaucracy in their daily lives and he reads the products of scholars who write about bureaucracy. He is still faced with the choice of a conceptual strategy when dealing with the phenomena to which the term 'bureaucracy' has been applied. It would, of course, be totally contrary to the spirit of the preceding account for this writer to attempt to offer an 'authoritative' new definition of bureaucracy. All that has gone before should indicate that this would be nugatory and self-defeating. But some comments on the respective merits of differing conceptual strategies may be in order.

If we consider the concepts we have reviewed in terms of their general use and acceptability, one factor stands out. The more clearly a concept has been articulated with a general conceptual framework, the greater likelihood it has of penetrating into the thinking of social scientists. Max Weber's, Harold Lasswell's or even John Stuart Mill's ideas of bureaucracy are not whims of the moment but are supported by a range of other concepts which, to a large extent, stand or fall together. A counsel of perfection to the would-be producer of the ultimate definition of bureaucracy might well be to ensure that his concept was part of a total and comprehensive conceptual framework for social science. But to take on such a task can only be viewed as quixotic. The number of such frameworks in existence seems to suggest that each new scheme will only be an addition to, rather than a replacement of, what exists already. Moreover, as we have seen, social change involves a constant revision of concepts and it is difficult to envisage any final and authoritative conceptual scheme.

A radically different approach is to consider the term 'bureaucracy' as it is used in everyday speech. Its wide currency has been remarked on ever since the 1840s. Social life is dependent on shared concepts and it may be felt that there is bound to be sufficient consensus about the meaning of bureaucracy in popular parlance to warrant acceptance of this concept by social scientists. The difficulties here are notorious. It is by no means certain that the popular use of the term invariably has an empirical referent. It may be no more informative than any other expostulation of anger, in which the use of words indicates more about the state of the individual using them than any aspect of a perceived situation. But even if we concentrate on those occasions when the term does refer clearly to an aspect of social life, we are faced with the same problem as we meet with in the most sophisticated social science concepts. For social science and social life are not hermetically sealed off from each other. We must expect the usages of academic discussion to percolate into everyday language, and we cannot anticipate some neutral arbitration between them.

A third strategy is designed to do precisely this—to provide a middle course between the various concepts. It was employed in the very first academic scrutiny of the concept of bureaucracy. In 1846 Robert von Mohl expressed his concern at the varying uses of the term 'bureaucracy'. Everyone, he said, is talking about it, yet no one appears to have given it thought. Many people, he thought, use it to demonstrate their intelligence, or to give the impression of insight and political sophistication. 'In these circumstances, the surest approach to a clear idea of this frequently used but ill-defined concept is to compile as comprehensive a list as possible of the various accounts of the tendencies and consequences of bureaucracy.'[4] He hoped to devise a definition, as a result of this compilation, which included only those elements on which there was general agreement.

This method still has its adherents, and we have come across examples of it.[5] But its successful employment is dependent on the validity of a basic assumption, which is that the varying definitions of a term are simply different attempts to sum up the specific nature of the same range of objects (*denotata*). Put in other terms, the premise is that different writers on bureaucracy are talking about the same thing and merely disagree on the appropriate language for describing it. Now if the account in this book is correct such an assumption must be invalid in the case of bureaucracy. For we have found quite distinct concepts using that name. Certainly these concepts overlap and we have concentrated on showing how they are related, logically and historically. But there is no element common to them all which could form part of a useful definition.

Clearly there seems to be only one possible approach left. This is to avoid the use of the term 'bureaucracy' while pursuing research in the areas in which it has been employed, for nothing in this book should be thought to diminish the importance of such work. Indeed the writer hopes that such conceptual clarification as he may have achieved will contribute to the success of future research. Such a course can, without doubt, save much confusion. But it is possible to salvage something small from the wrecks of these conceptual strategies. When we say that the concepts we have discussed are *related*, we may have found the major information function which the term 'bureaucracy' has.

To identify different groups of related human beings we have family names. They are devoid of meaning, but none the less useful. In the same way 'bureaucracy' is useful in identifying a range of related problems, i.e. the whole gamut of issues concerning the relations of individuals to abstract organizational features. We cannot expect this name to tell us anything more than the fact of relationship, of historical and logical connection between these problems. But that single piece of information is important enough, for academics and citizens alike.

Notes
and
References

Full publication details of works cited will be found in the Bibliography.

Introduction

1 *Parliamentary Debates, House of Commons Official Report*, Vol. 757, no. 48, January 29, 1968, col. 885, 'Growth of Bureaucracy'.
2 Ibid., col. 967. The speaker was Mr J. W. Pardoe, Liberal member for Cornwall, North.
3 Ibid., col. 980. Mr George Lawson, Labour member for Motherwell, replying to Sir Harmar Nicholls, Conservative member for Peterborough.
4 W. R. Sharp, "La Développement de la Bureaucratie aux États-Unis", *Revue des Sciences Politiques*, Vol. 50, 1927, p. 394.
5 F. Morstein Marx, 'Bureaucracy and Consultation', *Review of Politics*, Vol. 1, 1939, p. 87.
6 In *Reader in Bureaucracy*, edited by R. K. Merton et al., 1952, and *Bureaucracy and Bureaucratization*, a trend report and bibliography by S. N. Eisenstadt, 1958.

1/The Emergence of the Concept

1 Vincent de Gournay (1712–59) translated influential writers on economics, such as Child and Culpepper, into French. Himself an *intendant du commerce*, he was an important member of the group of economists known as the Physiocrats. For biographical details see G. Schelle, *Vincent de Gournay*, 1897.
2 Baron de Grimm and Diderot, *Correspondance, Littéraire, Philosphique et Critique*, 1753–69, 1813 edn, Vol. 4, p. 146. De Gournay's verbal inventiveness appears to have been considerable. The slogan, '*laissez faire, laissez passer*', has also been attributed to him.
3 Ibid., p. 508. Letter of July 15, 1765.
4 D. Warnotte in "Bureaucratie et Fonctionnairisme", 1937, recounts that de Gournay invented the term after a visit to Hamburg in 1745 but gives no source for this story.
5 N. Machiavelli, *The Prince*, Ch. 22.
6 See H. G. Creel, "The Beginnings of Bureaucracy in China: The Origin of the Hsien", 1964.
7 *Dictionnaire de la Langue Française*, Supplément, 1798.
8 J. H. Campe, *Wörterbuch zu Erklärung und Verdeutschung der unseren Sprache aufgedrungenen fremden Ausdrücke*, Braunschweig 1813, p. 161.
9 M. A. Marchi, *Dizionario Technico-Etimilogico-Filologico*, Milan 1828, p. 138.
10 Honoré de Balzac, *Les Employés*, 1836, translated by E. Marriage as *Bureaucracy*, 1898, p. 84.
11 F. Le Play, *La Réforme Sociale en France*, 1864, p. 237.
12 E. Littré, *Dictionnaire de la Langue Française*, Hachette, Paris 1873.
13 M. Block, *Petit Dictionnaire Politique et Social*, Perrin, Paris, 1896, p. 94.
14 H. Schulz, *Deutsches Fremdwörterbuch*, Trübner, Strassburg 1913, p. 102.

15   C. J. Kraus, *Vermischte Schriften*, Nicolovius, Königsberg 1808, p. 247.

16   W. von Humboldt, *Ideen zu einem Versuch die Gränzen der Wirksamkeit des Staats zu bestimmen*, first published 1851.

17   *Die Briefe des Freiherrn von Stein an den Freiherrn von Gagern 1813–1831*, Cotta, Stuttgart 1833, pp. 90–2, letter of August 24, 1821.

18   K. Heinzen, *Die Preussische Büreaukratie*, 1845, p. 11. It is worth noting Stein's emphasis on the caste nature of the bureaucrats. Marx was familiar with Heinzen's work and would have come across this passage by Stein in Heinzen, if not in the original.

19   J. J. von Görres, *Europa und die Revolution*, 1821, p. 149.

20   J. J. von Görres, *Deutschland und die Revolution*, 1819.

21   In the translation by J. Black (Longmans, London 1820) it was rendered as 'regulated on the principle of offices or bureaus' (p. 253). In the anonymous translation in *The Pamphleteer* (London 1820), it was omitted through abridgement.

22   *Tour in England, Ireland, and France*, by a German Prince (Prince von Pückler-Muskau), tr. by Mrs S. Austen, Effingham, Wilson, London 1832, p. 34.

23   *The Popular Encyclopaedia*, Blackie, Glasgow 1837, p. 755.

24   Thomas Carlyle, *Latter Day Pamphlets*, No. IV, "The New Downing Street", April 15, 1850, in *Collected Works*, Vol. 19, Chapman and Hall, London 1870, p. 173.

25   H. Spencer, *The Study of Sociology*, 1st edn 1837; 1961, p. 111.

26   Arnout O'Donnel, "State Education in France", p. 583.

27   J. S. Blackie, "Prussia and the Prussian System", passim.

28   J. S. Mill, *Principles of Political Economy*, Vol. 2, p. 528.

29   J. S. Mill, *On Liberty*, 1892 edn, p. 66.

30   J. S. Mill, *Considerations on Representative Government*, p. 113.

31   Ibid., p. 114.

32   Ibid., p. 115.

33   Ibid., p. 117.

34   W. Bagehot, *The English Constitution*, 1963 edn, p. 197.

35   Ibid., p. 198.

36   E. Fischel, *Die Verfassung Englands*, 1862, pp. 132–6 and 249–52.

37   F. von Schulte, "Bureaucracy and its Operation in Germany and Austria-Hungary", p. 456.

38   Ibid., p. 432.

39   Ibid., p. 458.

40   Ibid., p. 433.

41   See A. Lang, *Life, Letters and Diaries of Sir Stafford Northcote*, Blackwood, Edinburgh and London 1890, Vol. 2, p. 219.

42   Published in book form the following year as *The Man versus the State*, they were entitled "The New Toryism", "The Coming Slavery", "The Sins of the Legislators", and "The Great Political Superstition".

43   H. Spencer, *The Man versus the State*, p. 33. In an essay of 1871, "Specialized Administration", Spencer outlined his theory of the negative role of the state and his absolute opposition to positive interference.

44   F. C. Montague, *The Limits of Individual Liberty*, p. 229.

45   A. S. Green, "Growing Bureaucracy and Parliamentary Decline", 1900.

46   "The Encroaching Bureaucracy" (anonymous), *The Quarterly Review*, 1917, p. 52.

47   J. Ramsay Muir, *Peers and Bureaucrats*, p. 8.

48   Ibid., p. 14.

49 Ibid., p. 22.
50 L. von Stein, *Die Verwaltungslehre*, 2nd edn 1869, p. 14.
51 A good source in English is H. C. Johnson's "Concept of Bureaucracy in Cameralism", 1964. This is somewhat unhappily titled since, as the author states, the term 'bureaucracy' was not current in the writing he discusses, and indeed the German concept of bureaucracy was developed to highlight a contrast with cameralist thinking.
52 See in particular the frequently cited text by a Westphalian finance minister, C. A. von Malchus, *Politik der inneren Staatsverwaltung*, 1823, especially pp. 5–8.
53 *Allgemeine deutsche Real-Encyclopaedie oder Conversationslexikon*, Brockhaus, Leipzig, 5th edn 1819, Vol. 2, p. 158.
54 Heinzen, op. cit., p. 12.
55 F. Rohmer, *Deutschlands alte und neue Bureaukratie*, 1848, p. 1. An anonymous article of 1857, "Der bureaukratische Staat nach seinem Ausgangspunkt und Ziel", offered yet another solution to bureaucracy in the form of a society based on professional groups.
56 As, for instance, in *Das Staatslexicon*, edited by K. von Rotteck and K. Welcker, 1859, and *Deutsches Staatswörterbuch*, edited by J. C. Bluntschli and K. Brater, 1857.
57 *Conversationslexicon*, Brockhaus, Leipzig 1864, Vol. 3, pp. 873–4.
58 Stein, op. cit., p. 287.
59 R. von Mohl, "Ueber Bureaukratie", 1862 edn, claims that after 1846 everyone began to discuss this topic.
60 Ibid., p. 108.
61 K. Brater, in Bluntschli and Brater, op. cit., p. 294 strongly deprecated this usage.
62 J. Olszewski, *Bureaukratie*, 1904. This volume has gone unnoticed in the Anglo-Saxon literature. It appears to be the first separate volume devoted wholly to the topic of bureaucracy, but a full length study entitled "La Burocrazia e il Governo Parlamentare", by I. Santangelo Spoto appeared two years earlier in the *Biblioteca di Scienze Politiche e Amministrative*, edited by A. Brunialti. Relying largely on the sources discussed in this chapter, this study is concerned with the genesis and structure of bureaucracy, its organization in Italy and France, its reform, and the idea of responsible bureaucracy.
63 F. Le Play, op. cit., pp. 236–5.
64 For instance L. Vivien's *Études Administratives*, 1845, makes no reference to the problem.
65 A. de Tocqueville, *L'Ancien Régime et la Révolution*, 8th edn 1877, p. 246.
66 P. Leroy-Beaulieu, *L'État Moderne et ses Fonctions*, especially p. 49 and pp. 80–8.

2/The Classical Formulations

1 The edition was dated 1896.
2 In his *Sulla Teorica dei Governi e sul Governo Parlamentare*, 1884, Ch. 1.
3 Ibid., p. 18.
4 *Storia delle Dottrine Politiche*, 1933, Ch. 40. An English translation of this chapter is given by J. H. Meisel at the end of *The Myth of the Ruling Class*, 1958.
5 See "The Anti-Aristotelianism of Gaetano Mosca and its Fate", by R. Sereno in *Ethics*, Vol. 48, 1937–38.

6   *Sulla Teorica*, p. 19 as translated by Meisel, op. cit., p. 32.

7   In the *Storia* he added the city state to make a third type.

8   The importance Mosca attached to bureaucracy was a feature of *The Ruling Class* which represented a novel development compared with his earlier *Sulla Teorica*. As Meisel (op. cit., p. 137), says, it was introduced 'rather suddenly'. It is not possible to ascertain what, if any, new influences had affected Mosca.

9   The last six chapters of the English edition of *The Ruling Class* were written in 1920–23. These were especially marked by their opposition to bureaucratic rule, but it is also evident in the earlier chapters.

10 *The Ruling Class*, pp. 142–3. Subsequently (p. 284) Mosca said, 'Communist and collectivist societies would beyond any doubt be managed by officials'. This successful prediction should encourage all who despair of the predictive powers of social science.

11 Ibid., p. 134.

12 Ibid., p. 269.

13 As Meisel points out (op. cit., pp. 196–206) Mosca never bothered to define bureaucracy and he neglected Max Weber and his school.

14 Mosca, op. cit., pp. 83–4.

15 Published in German as *Zur Soziologie des Parteiwesens in der modernen Demokratie.*

16 Mosca, op. cit., p. 365.

17 Ibid., p. 338.

18 The fatalism of Michels's approach as compared with Mosca's was reflected in their political careers. Believing oligarchy inevitable Michels supported the Fascists in Italy, whereas Mosca never joined them.

19 See above, p. 32.

20 The best account of Weber's substantive sociological work is that of R. Bendix, *Max Weber, An Intellectual Portrait*, 1960.

21 The first, "Wesen, Voraussetzungen und Entfaltung der bürokratischen Herrschaft", stemmed from the years 1911–13 and appeared on pp. 559–87 of *Wirtschaft und Gesellschaft* 4th edn (cited henceforward as *WuG*). It has been translated by H. H. Gerth and C. Wright Mills on pp. 196–244 of their selection *From Max Weber: Essays in Sociology*, 1948. The second, written between 1918–20, appeared in *WuG*, pp. 125–30. It has been translated by A. M. Henderson and T. Parsons in *The Theory of Social and Economic Organisation*, 1947, pp. 329–41.

22 "Parlament und Regierung im neugeordneten Deutschland", was reprinted in Max Weber's *Gesammelte Politische Schriften*, 2nd edn 1958, pp. 294–431 (henceforward referred to as *GPS*).

23 A very recent example of emphasis upon the methodology of Weber's writing on bureaucracy is N. Mouzelis, *Organization and Bureaucracy*, 1967. For an article interpreting Weber's theory as an expression of a philosophy of history see A. Gouldner, "Metaphysical Pathos and the Theory of Bureaucracy", *American Political Science Review*, Vol. 49, 1955. This issue will be discussed further in the next chapter.

24 In Henderson and Parsons, op. cit., see pp. 145–52.

25 Henderson and Parsons translate *Verband* as 'corporate group'. This sounds too legalistic to this writer. *Verband* is as common a term in German as organization is in English.

26 Henderson and Parsons, op. cit., p. 150.

27 Ibid., p. 146.

28 *WuG*, p. 545. Cf. M. Rheinstein, *Max Weber on Law in Economy and Society*, 1954, p. 330.

29 Henderson and Parsons, op. cit., p. 152. Parsons notes 'the term *Herrschaft* has no satisfactory English equivalent'. Rheinstein prefers to translate it as 'domination'. The nearest translation is 'rule' as in 'rule of kings', but unfortunately 'rule' has another meaning as in of 'rules of the game'. 'Authority' seems the best translation since Weber himself, *WuG*, p. 544 used *Autoritat* as a synonym for his special meaning of *Herrschaft*.

30 *WuG*, p. 28. Cf. Henderson and Parsons, op. cit., p. 152.

31 *WuG*, p. 28.

32 Rheinstein, op. cit., p. 330, *WuG*, p. 541.

33 *WuG*, p. 28, Henderson and Parsons, op. cit., p. 152.

34 *WuG*, p. 548, translated in Rheinstein, op. cit., p. 334. He referred to 'the so-called "advantage of the small number" '.

35 *WuG*, p. 153. Cf. Henderson and Parsons, op. cit., p. 382.

36 Weber outlined this scheme several times: *WuG*, pp. 122–57, translated by Henderson and Parsons, op. cit., pp. 324–92; *WuG*, pp. 549–50, translated by Rheinstein, op. cit., pp. 336–7; *WuG*, pp. 551–8.

37 e.g. *WuG*, p. 126, p. 550.

38 *WuG*, p. 127; Henderson and Parsons, op. cit., p. 335; *GPS*, p. 319.

39 e.g. *WuG*, pp. 126, 552.

40 *GPS*, pp. 308–10.

41 *WuG*, p. 552.

42 *WuG*, p. 552.

43 A very good, brief summary of these is available in R. Aron, *Main Currents in Sociological Thought*, Vol. 2, 1967, pp. 197–204.

44 The following version of Weber's ideal typical formulation on legal authority and a bureaucratic administrative staff is taken from *WuG*, pp. 124–8. For a translation see Henderson and Parsons, op. cit., pp. 329–34.

45 These propositions are also set out in abbreviated form.

46 *WuG*, pp. 126–7; Henderson and Parsons, op. cit., p. 334.

47 *WuG*, p. 128; Henderson and Parsons, op. cit., p. 337.

48 e.g. *GPS*, pp. 318, 321.

49 *GPS*, p. 310.

50 *WuG*, pp. 154, 564.

51 Ibid., pp. 158–76; Henderson and Parsons, op. cit., pp. 392–423. These were apart from the legal definition of the rights and duties of the bureaucrats.

52 As early as 1895, in his inaugural lecture, Weber had taken 'national power' as a political good of paramount importance. The extent of Weber's nationalism and responsibility for later developments in Germany have become a matter for heated debate.

3/The Debate with Weber

1 For an account see A. Oberschall, *Empirical Social Research in Germany, 1848–1914*, pp. 134–6, where the author also refers to Weber's non-ideal type of bureaucracy.

2 In *Il Pensiero Moderno*, Vol. 1, 1912, pp. 310–16, cited by J. H. Meisel, op. cit.

3 *From Max Weber*, edited by H. H. Gerth and C. Wright Mills, 1948, p. 232.

4 Ibid., p. 232. A good account of the careful consideration Weber gave to the problem of power and bureaucracy is A. Diamant's "The Bureaucratic

Model: Max Weber Rejected, Rediscovered, Reformed", in *Papers in Comparative Public Administration*, edited by F. Heady and S. L. Stokes, 1962.

5 "Die Behördenorganisation und die allgemeine Staatsverwaltung Preussens im 18 Jahrhundert", in *Acta Borussica*, Vol. I and "Der deutsche Beamten-staat vom 16 bis 18 Jahrhundert", in *Umrisse und Untersuchungen zur Verfassungs- Verwaltungs- und Wirtschaftsgeschichte*, 1898.

6 Schmoller, "Die Behördenorganisation", p. 31 (this author's translation).

7 Ibid., p. 32.

8 E. Strauss, *The Ruling Servants*, 1961, pp. 40–1.

9 Available in his *Reader in Bureaucracy*, 1952, pp. 361–71.

10 Ibid., p. 362.

11 The major statement of his theory is in *TVA and the Grass Roots*, 1949. An earlier version is contained in his "An Approach to a Theory of Bureau-cracy", in the *American Sociological Review*, 1943.

12 For a useful account of these see G. Friedman, *Industrial Society*, 1955.

13 Henderson and Parsons, op. cit., pp. 58–60.

14 Gouldner also mentions a third type, mock-bureaucracy, where the rules are not taken seriously by any of the participants.

15 In *Verfassung und Verfassungsrecht*, reprinted in *Staats rechtliche Abhand-lungen und andere Aufsätze*, 1955, p. 30 (this author's translation).

16 See "Bureaucracy: the Problem and its Setting", in the *American Soci-ological Review*, 1947.

17 R. Bendix, *Higher Civil Servants in American Society*, p. 12.

18 "Some Observations on Weber's Analysis of Bureaucracy", in R. K. Merton, *Reader in Bureaucracy*, 1952, p. 31.

19 "Theoretical Limitations of Max Weber's Systematic Analysis of Bureau-cracy", in the *Philippine Journal of Public Administration*, 1957.

20 P. M. Blau, *The Dynamics of Bureaucracy*, p. 201.

21 "Bureaucratic and Craft Administration of Production: A Comparative Study", *Administrative Science Quarterly*, 1959–60.

22 See G. Sjöberg, R. A. Brymer and B. Farris, "Bureaucracy and the Lower Class", in *Sociology and Social Research*, 1966.

23 See E. Litwak and H. J. Meyer, "A Balance Theory of Co-ordination be-tween Bureaucratic Organisations and Community Primary Groups", in *Administrative Science Quarterly*, 1966–67.

24 In "Weberian v. Welfare Bureaucracy in Traditional Society", *Adminis-trative Science Quarterly*, 1961–62.

25 "The Development and Decline of Patrimonial and Bureaucratic Adminis-trations", *Administrative Science Quarterly*, 1962–63.

26 See his introduction to that volume, "An Overview of Bureaucracy and Political Development".

27 "Metaphysical Pathos and the Theory of Bureaucracy", *American Political Science Review*, 1955.

28 "Max Weber's Two Conceptions of Bureaucracy", *American Journal of Sociology*, 1957–58.

29 "Max Weber et La Russie", *Le Contrat Social*, 1960. Similarly F. S. Burin has argued that Weber would not have been able to account for the Nazi party's subversion of the German civil service (in "Bureaucracy and National Socialism: A Reconsideration of Weberian Theory", in R. K. Merton's *Reader in Bureaucracy*, 1952).

30 "The Beginnings of Bureaucracy in China: The Origin of the Hsien", *Journal of Asian Studies*, 1964.

31 "The Bureaucrat as Pro-Consul: The Restoration Prefect and the Police Generale", *Comparative Studies in Society and History*, 1965.

32 M. Berger, *Bureaucracy and Society in Modern Egypt*, 1957 and C. Beck, 'Bureaucracy and Political Development in Eastern Europe" in La Palombara, op. cit., 1963.

33 See above, note 18.

34 As examples of this point of view one may mention S. R. Udy, "Bureaucracy and Rationality in Weber's Organisation Theory", *American Sociological Review*, 1959; R. H. Hall, "The Concept of Bureaucracy—an Empirical Assessment", *American Journal of Sociology*, 1963; C. R. Hinings et al., "An Approach to the Study of Bureaucracy", *Sociology*, 1967.

35 Blau and Scott, op. cit., p. 534.

36 For a more recent restatement of this view see N. Mouzelis, *Organisation and Bureaucracy*, 1967.

37 March and Simon, op. cit., p. 36.

38 R. G. Francis and R. C. Stone, *Service and Procedure in Bureaucracy*, p. 7.

39 Mouzelis, op. cit., p. 51.

40 "Max Weber's Ideal typus der Bürokratie und die Organisationssoziologie", *Kölner Zeitschrift für Soziologie und Sozialpsychologie*, 1965.

41 "Rationality" or a cognate term appears on twenty-three occasions even in the briefest of Weber's three essays on bureaucracy.

42 *WuG*, p. 124; Henderson and Parsons, op. cit., p. 328.

43 *WuG*, p. 125; Henderson and Parsons, op. cit., p. 329. This was the first of Weber's five propositions on the basis of legal authority (see above p. 43). Weber used his two technical terms, *Zweckrationalität* (purposive rationality) and *Wertrationalitat* (value rationality), to express the difference between laws which were means to ends and laws which were the direct embodiment of values.

44 *WuG*, p. 125; Henderson and Parsons, op. cit., p. 330. This was the second of his five propositions.

45 *WuG*, p. 125; Henderson and Parsons, op. cit., p. 330. This was the fifth of the five propositions.

46 *WuG*, p. 126; Henderson and Parson, op. cit., 331. Parson notes that he finds this distinction unclarified by Weber. It is best understood as the institutional counterpart of Weber's two types of rational action.

47 *WuG*, p. 126; Henderson and Parsons, op. cit., p. 331.

48 *WuG*, p. 129; Henderson and Parsons, op. cit., p. 339.

49 *WuG*, p. 141; Henderson and Parsons, op. cit., p. 361.

50 This was especially true of the Germany of Weber's time. Even today the majority of higher civil servants in Germany are trained lawyers. But, of course, even in countries without systems of administrative law the interpretation of laws and regulations is an important part of administrative activity.

51 Weber sometimes termed this the 'paradox of consequences' (*Paradoxie der Folgen*). Merton's "Bureaucratic Structure and Personality" does at least acknowledge the importance of this idea and Weber's emphasis on it. It is ironic that it should have been used in criticism of Weber.

52 See E. Baumgarten, *Max Weber: Werk und Person*, 1964, p. 514.

53 Ibid., p. 516.

54 It is, therefore, not without significance that Mayntz (see above, note 40), finds it necessary to attribute to Weber a concern for *'Effizienz'*, a word he did not use.

55 A good example of the over-eagerness of writers in English to make an issue out of Weber's supposed concern for efficiency is provided by Gouldner in the introduction to *Patterns of Industrial Bureaucracy*, pp. 19–21. He assumes Weber was discussing what made bureaucracy effective. But the quotation he takes for criticism involves an altogether unwarranted insertion of the idea of effectiveness by the translator.

56 For a discussion of the difficulties see the entry on 'efficiency' in *A Dictionary of the Social Sciences*, edited by J. Gould and W. L. Kolb, 1964.

57 Implicit in Weber's distinction was the difference between the rationality of thought and the rationality of conduct. A similar distinction in a different context has recently been made by I. C. Jarvie and J. Agassi, "The Problem of the Rationality of Magic" in the *British Journal of Sociology*, 1967.

58 See above, p. 61.

59 Thus Weber viewed the Taylor theories of management as a contribution to rationalizing production. See Henderson and Parsons, op. cit., p. 261.

60 See "Der Beamte", an essay reprinted in *Ideen zur Stats-und Kulturzoziologie*, 1927.

61 The best statement of Weber's position is contained in Herbert Sultan's essay "Bürokratie und Politische Machtbildung", 1955. He makes a point of explaining the small part the problem of inefficiency played in Weber's conceptualization of bureaucracy.

4/Bureaucracy and the Ideologists

1 In the *Marx-Engels Gesamtausgabe* (henceforward cited as MEGA), Section 1, Vol. 1. The relevant section, "Die Regierungsgewalt", is on pp. 448–64.

2 Hegel's *Philosophy of Right*, translated by T. M. Knox, 1942, p. 193.

3 P. Naville, *Le Nouveau Leviathan*, 1957, p. 98.

4 MEGA, p. 456: 'The bureaucratic spirit is an out and out jesuitical, theological spirit. The bureaucrats are the state Jesuits and state theologians. Bureaucracy is *la république pretre*.'

5 Ibid., p. 457.

6 K. Marx and F. Engels, *The German Ideology*, p. 78.

7 In *Marx and Engels: Basic Writings on Politics and Philosophy*, edited by L. S. Feuer, 1959, p. 29.

8 Ibid., p. 127.

9 Ibid., p. 456. For Heinzen, see above Ch. 1, p. 28.

10 Naville, op. cit., p. 101, says that at this stage Marx was still a democrat and not yet a communist.

11 Marx and Engels, *The German Ideology*, pp. 208–9.

12 In an article in the *Neue Rheinische Zeitung*, November 12, 1848, "Die Kontrerevolution in Berlin", reprinted in MEGA, Section 7, Vol. 1, p. 430.

13 Feuer, op. cit., p. 343.

14 Ibid., p. 343.

15 Ibid., p. 29.

16 For Bakunin's views on bureaucracy see G. P. Maximoff, *The Political Philosophy of Bakunin: Scientific Anarchism*.

17 K. Wittfogel, "The Ruling Bureaucracy of Oriental Despotism. A Phenomenon that Paralyzed Marx", *Review of Politics*, Vol. 15, 1953. S. Avineri, *The Social and Political Thought of Karl Marx*, 1968, p. 51, records an instance where Marx spoke of India being ruled by a bureaucracy. But this is insufficient to warrant rejecting Wittfogel's interpretation, which is shared by G. Lichtheim, *Marxism*, 1961, p. 384.

18 *One Step Forward, Two Steps Back*, quoted in T. Anderson, *Masters of Russian Marxism*, 1963, p. 66.

19 *Die Voraussetzungen des Sozialismus und die Aufgaben der Sozialdemokratie*, 1899, translated as *Evolutionary Socialism*, 1909, p. 55.

20 "Leninism or Marxism?", 1904, in *The Russian Revolution and Leninism and Marxism*, edited by B. D. Wolfe, 1961, p. 102.

21 Ibid., "The Russian Revolution", 1918, p. 71.

22 *The Labour Revolution*, 1925, includes a chapter devoted to bureaucracy.

23 *Collected Works*, Vol. 25, 1964, pp. 486–7.

24 Ibid., p. 481.

25 Ibid., pp. 486–7.

26 See R. V. Daniels, *The Conscience of the Revolution: Communist Opposition in Soviet Russia*, 1960, pp. 115–8.

27 Ibid., p. 145.

28 See T. Anderson, op. cit., pp. 179–88.

29 See A. G. Meyer, *Leninism*, 1957, p. 214.

30 J. Stalin, *Leninism*, 1928, Vol. 2, pp. 372–3.

31 See A. Brumberg, "Soviet Campaign against Survivals of Capitalism", *Russian Review*, Vol. 12, 1953.

32 See K. P. Mangold, "Lenin's Cardinal Rules of Poverty and Recall: Neglected Ideological Weapons for the West", *Orbis*, Vol. 8, 1964–5.

33 MEGA, Section I, Vol. III, "Kritische Randglossen zu dem Artikel: 'Der König vom Preussen und die Sozialreform. Von einem Preussen' ", 1844, p. 14.

34 G. D. H. Cole sees bureaucratization as the real issue between Trotsky and Stalin in his *History of Socialist Thought*, Vol. 4, 1963, p. 861.

35 *The New Course*, translated by M. Schachtman, 1943, pp. 50–1.

36 *The Revolution Betrayed*, p. 235.

37 Published under the pseudonym Bruno R.

38 Published in a collected edition as *The Bureaucratic Revolution: The Rise of the Stalinist State*, 1962.

39 'Mussolini's and Hitler's regimes have come to be essentially similar to Stalin's. . . . The rest is choreography.' Rizzi, op. cit., p. 314.

40 This did not prevent Rizzi from calling for a proletarian revolution to replace the existing bureaucracy with a new directing class.

41 See J. Djordevic, "Local Self-Government in Yugoslavia", *American Slavic and East European Review*, Vol. 12, 1953.

42 *State and Law: Soviet and Yugoslav Theory*, 1964, p. 50.

43 *The Thoughts of Chairman Mao Tse-tung*, 1967, especially pp. 24, 30, 35, 74–5, 80 and 174. Chen Po-Ta, in *Mao Tse-tung on the Chinese Revolution*, 1953, pp. 25–6, notes the importance of the element 'bureaucratic-capitalism' in Mao's revolutionary formula.

44 See *Cuba, Socialisme et Développement*, 1964, p. 108. He has also written on the theme of Cuba and bureaucracy in *Lands Alive*, 1965, Ch. 7.

45 As reported by Theodore Draper, *Castroism, Theory and Practice*, 1965, pp. 192–7, where he gives an account of the dispute between a French Communist, Charles Bettelheim, and Che Guevara.

46 *Marxism in Modern France*, 1966, pp. 182–90.

47 See J. Sauvageot, A. Geismar, D. Cohn-Bendit, and J.-P. Duteuil, *The Student Revolt*, 1968, p. 60. Geismar is speaking.

48 Ibid., p. 79.

49 For the United States see *The New Radicals*, edited by P. Jacobs and S. Landau, 1966, especially the sixth section, "The FSM—Revolt against Liberal Bureaucracy".

50 An additional exception can be made of Bukharin who was familiar with some sociology, in particular that of Michels. The nearest approach to a critical analysis of the concept of bureaucracy among Marxists is to be found in André Stawar's *Libres Essais Marxistes*, 1963. His essay "La Bureaucratie Soviétique" dates from 1934. He was under the surveillance of both his own government in Poland and the Stalinists.

51 Good accounts of the response of the Fascists to bureaucracy will be found in S. Neumann, *Permanent Revolution*, 1942; Franz Neumann, *Behemoth, The Structure and Practice of National Socialism*, 1942; F. Morstein Marx, "Bureaucracy and Dictatorship", *Review of Politics*, 1941.

52 This is the view of Franz Neumann, op. cit., p. 39.

53 B. Mussolini, *The Doctrine of Fascism*, 1935, p. 12.

54 A. Hitler, *Mein Kampf*, p. 154. Similar statements can also be found in Alfred Rosenberg's work, e.g. in *Der Mythus des 20 Jahrhunderts*, 1930, 1943 edn, p. 526.

55 Quoted by Franz Neumann, op. cit., p. 68.

56 B. Mussolini, *My Autobiography*, n.d., p. 268.

57 B. Mussolini, *The Corporate State*, 1938, p. 28.

58 For an account of Mussolini's methods see T. Cole, "Italy's Fascist Bureaucracy", *American Political Science Review*, 1938.

59 B. Mussolini, *The Corporate State*, p. 46. Both capitalist and socialist systems were going in this direction according to Mussolini; something of an anticipation of Rizzi's position.

60 Hitler, op. cit., pp. 119, 156–7.

61 See for example F. Morstein Marx, "German Bureaucracy in Transition", *American Political Science Review*, 1934; F. S. Burin, "Bureaucracy and National Socialism—a Reconsideration of Weberian Theory", in R. K. Merton et al., *Reader in Bureaucracy*, 1952.

62 *Blut und Ehre*, 1936, Vol. 2, p. 68.

63 See his "Legalität und Legitimität", 1932, reprinted in *Verfassungsrechtliche Aufsätze 1924–54*, 1958.

64 Examples include J. M. Beck, *Our Wonderland of Bureaucracy*, 1932; J. H. Crider, *The Bureaucrat*, 1944; L. Sullivan, *The Dead Hand of Bureaucracy*, 1940; and *Bureaucracy Runs Amuck*, 1944.

65 E. Pendelton Herring, *Public Administration and the Public Interest*, p. 15. Hermann Finer, "Critics of 'Bureaucracy'", *Political Science Quarterly*, 1945, also attacks these writers on bureaucracy for their indiscriminate use of the term.

66 L. von Mises, *Bureaucracy*, 1946, p.2.

67 J. A. Schumpeter, *Capitalism, Socialism and Democracy*, third edn 1950, p. 206.

68 For a good survey of the attitudes of various socialists to bureaucracy see R. Bendix, "Socialism and the Theory of Bureaucracy", *Canadian Journal of Economic and Political Science*, 1950. A book as influential as C. A. R. Crosland's *The Future of Socialism*, 1956, omits any discussion of the problem.

69 "The Future of Politics", three articles in *The Guardian*, January 8, 9, 10, 1968, the quotation coming from the first, "Bureaucrats in the Saddle".

5/Seven Modern Concepts of Bureaucracy

1 Examples of this *tabula rasa* approach include G. Tullock's *The Politics of Bureaucracy*, 1965, and A. Downs' "Theory of Bureaucracy", *American Economic Review*, Vol. 55, 1965.

2   They will also be discussed in the concluding chapter.

3   N. Mouzelis, op. cit., pp. 4, 54; J. P. Nettl, op. cit., p. 337.

4   Mouzelis uses 'bureaucracy as Weber did, that is only as an extreme type' (p. 54). Nettl defines bureaucracy 'in a Weberian sense—as a phenomenon of modernity but not necessarily as the product of, or synonymous with, organizational and even social rationality' (p. 337).

5   It should, of course, be borne in mind in the following discussion that the seven concepts which are distinguished are not always held in pure form. Almost any combination of them is possible, but for the sake of clarity we shall concentrate on the pure types.

6   P. Blau, *The Dynamics of Bureaucracy*, rev. edn, 1963, p. 251.

7   p. 60.

8   p. 8.

9   R. G. Francis and R. C. Stone, *Service and Procedure in Bureaucracy*, 1596, p. 3.

10 P. Leonard, *Sociology in Social Work*, 1966, p. 81.

11 Both Leonard and Francis and Stone use this terminology.

12 Thus Rosemary Stewart in *The Reality of Management*, 1963, p. 8, says that the characteristics of bureaucracy have developed 'because they are the most efficient method yet discovered of running a large organization'.

13 For examples of attempts to define non-Western forms of organizational rationality see C. K. Yang, "Some Characteristics of Chinese Bureaucratic Behaviour", in *Confucianism in Action*, edited by D. S. Nivison and A. F. Wright, 1959, and B. S. Silberman, "Bureaucracy and Economic Development in Japan", Vol. 5, 1965.

14 P. M. Blau, op. cit., 1st edn, p. 201.

15 For an attempt to show the differences of approach between the sociology of organizations and the normative perspective of organization theory, see Martin Albrow, "The Study of Organizations—Objectivity or Bias?", *Penguin Social Sciences Survey 1968*.

16 D. E. Apter and R. A. Lystad speak of bureaucracies where there is 'heavy emphasis on administrative efficiency', "Bureaucracy, Party and Constitutional Democracy: An Examination of Political Role Systems in Ghana', in G. M. Carter and W. O. Brown, *Transitive in Africa: Studies in Political Adaptation*, 1958, p. 20. This is some indication of the desire to preserve the distinction between the observer's view and the participant's logic.

17 M. E. Dimock, "Bureaucracy Self-examined", *Public Administration Review*, Vol. 4, 1944, p. 198. However in *Administration Vitality*, 1960, p. 4, he offers a different concept of bureaucracy: "the ordering of institutional management to secure the advantages of system'.

18 E. Strauss, op. cit., p. 41.

19 M. Crozier, op. cit., p. 187.

20 Both Blau and Crozier are committed to the language of function and dysfunction. It has often been remarked how easily this turns into a language of social criticism.

21 See Carl A. Emge, "Bürokratisierung unter Philosophischer und Soziologischer Sicht", *Kölner Zeitschrift für Soziologie*, Vol. 3, 1950–1, and Otto Stammer, "Bürokratie", in *Handbuch der Soziologie*, edited by W. Ziegenfuss, 1956.

22 p. 70.

23 See, in particular, his articles "Le 'Service Civil' en Angleterre", *Revue des Sciences Politiques*, Vol. 50, 1927; "Critics of 'bureaucracy' ", *Political Science Quarterly*, Vol. 60, 1945.

24 "La Développement de la Bureaucratie aux États-Unis", *Revue des Sciences Politiques*, Vol. 50, 1927, p. 394.

25 "Bureaucratie et Fonctionnairisme", *Revue de l'Institut de Sociologie Université libre de Bruxelles*, Vol. 17, 1937.

26 In *Annals of the American Academy of Political and Social Science*, Vol. 292, 1954.

27 p. 209.

28 p. 62.

29 F. Morstein Marx discusses Italian Fascism in "Bureaucracy and Dictatorship", *Review of Politics*, Vol. 3, 1941.

30 p. 3.

31 This distinction is also made by Onofre D. Corpuz in *The Bureaucracy in the Philippines*, 1957, p. 22. He adds that those who see bureaucracy as an apparatus tend also to see it as a juggernaut, while those who view it as a collection of individuals see it as more fragile. 'Particular analytical concepts of bureaucracy unavoidably affect conclusions' (p. 24).

32 These propositions are in "Levels of Economic Performance and Bureaucratic Structure" by B. F. Hoselitz in J. La Palombara, op. cit., pp. 171, 198.

33 In Ch. 4, "Types of Bureaucracy".

34 p. 157.

35 "The Bureaucracy and Political Development in Vietnam", La Palombara, op. cit., p. 322.

36 p. 7. In the same volume M. Fainsod, "Bureaucracy and Modernization: The Russian and Soviet Case", suggests a five-fold typology of bureaucracies: representative, party-state, military dominated, ruler dominated, ruling.

37 In *Toward the Comparative Study of Public Administration*, edited by W. J. Siffin, 1957.

38 Ibid., p. 26.

39 Ibid., p. 87.

40 Riggs, op. cit., p. 54.

41 "Bureaucracy and Political Development: A Paradoxical View", La Palombara, op. cit., p. 122.

42 *A Systems Analysis of Political Life*, 1964, pp. 212–20.

43 p. 45.

44 An early use of this concept is by O. H. Gablentz, "Industriebürokratie", *Schmollers Jahrbuch*, Vol. 50, 1926.

45 In H. Sultan and W. Abendroth, *Bürokratische Verwaltungsstaat und Soziale Demokratie*.

46 See above, p. 87. It is also the concept used by H. Cohen in *The Demonics of Bureaucracy*, 1965, a replication of part of Blau's *The Dynamics of Bureaucracy*.

47 p. 459.

48 "Bureaucracies: Some Contrasts in Systems", *Indian Journal of Public Administration*, Vol. 10, 1964.

49 See above, p. 58. Stinchcombe's suggestion is taken up in S. W. Becker's and G. Gordon's "An Entrepreneurial Theory of Formal Organizations, *Administrative Science Quarterly*, Vol. 11, 1966–67.

50 See above, p. 60.

51 H. Stroup, *Bureaucracy in Higher Education*, 1966, Preface.

52 p. 2.

53 C. S. Hyneman, *Bureaucracy in a Democracy*, 1950, p. 3; H. Simon, "Staff and Management Controls", *The Annals of the American Academy of Political and Social Science*, Vol. 292, 1954, p. 95; R. V. Presthus, *The Organizational Society*, 1965, p. 4; A. Etzioni, *Modern Organizations*, 1964, p. 3.

54 Ferrel Heady, *Public Administration: a Comparative Perspective*, 1966, p. 19.

55 Presthus, op. cit., p. 58; W. Bennis, "The Coming Death of Bureaucracy", in *Behaviour in Organizations: A Multidimensional View*, 1968, p. 257; Heady, op. cit., p. 20. For another such list see R. A. Dahl and C. E. Lindblom, *Politics, Economics and Welfare*, 1953, pp. 235–6.

56 See R. H. Hall, "The Concept of Bureaucracy: An Empirical Assessment", *American Journal of Sociology*, 1963.

57 Thus one group of researchers has reduced the idea of bureaucracy to theoretical insignificance and advocates the measurement of organizational dimensions without any prejudgement as to their shape. See C. R. Hinings et al. "An Approach to the Study of Bureaucracy", *Sociology*, Vol. 1, 1967.

58 p. 147.

59 See C. T. Schmidt, *The Corporate State in Action: Italy under Fascism*, 1939, especially pp. 69, 134.

60 *Freedom, Power and Democratic Planning*, 1951, p. 43.

61 Ibid., p. 44.

62 The idea of a bureaucratic culture is developed by Max Handman, "The Bureaucratic Culture Pattern and Political Revolutions", *American Journal of Sociology*, 1933. But he uses it for societies which are the lesser developed in the Western world.

63 pp. 4, 94.

64 See Gablentz, note 44 above, and E. Landauer, "Kapitalistischer Geist und Verwaltungsbürokratie in Öffentlichen Unternehmungen", *Schmollers Jahrbuch*, 54, 1930. R. Bendix regards it this way too in *Work and Authority in Industry*, 1956, especially in chapter 4.

65 "Bürokratisierung", *Kölner Zeitschrift für Soziologie*, Vol. 3, p. 196.

66 "Bureaucracy and Bureaucratization", *Current Sociology*, Vol. 7, 1958, p. 111.

67 Gehlen, op. cit., offers, p. 196, as a definition of bureaucratization, 'the process of for ever incorporating new elements into the administrative machine'.

6/Bureaucracy and the Theorists of Democracy

1 "Critics of 'Bureaucracy'", *Political Science Quarterly*, Vol. 60, 1945, p. 105.

2 The whole of the preceding discussion owes much to Max Weber's exposition of the relation between facts and values in social science, which is to be found in his essays published as *The Methodology of the Social Sciences*, translated and edited by E. A. Shils and H.A. Finch, 1949.

3 See J. Djordeyic, "Local Self-Government in Yugoslavia", *American Slavic and East European Review*, Vol. 12, 1953.

4 Thus Lasswell and Kaplan's typology of types of rule is formulated in neutral terms and excludes the category of democracy, preferring 'demosocracy'. See *Power and Society*, p. 207.

5 A useful account of delegated legislation in Britain is contained in G. A. Campbell's, *The Civil Service in Britain*, 1955, pp. 102–24.

6 J. M. Beck, op. cit., p. 23.

7 See C. K. Allen, *Bureaucracy Triumphant*, 1931; G. W. Keeton, *The Passing of Parliament*, 1952; L. Sullivan, *The Dead Hand of Bureaucracy*, 1940, and *Bureaucracy Runs Amuck*, 1944, in which the author finds the British Fabian socialists influencing the American Office of Price Administration, p. 176.

8 See Herman Finer, "Administrative Responsibility in Democratic Government", *Public Administration Review*, Vol. 1, 1941.

9 C. J. Friedrich, "Public Policy and the Nature of Administrative Responsibility", in *Public Policy*, edited by C. J. Friedrich and E. S. Mason, 1940. Both this essay and the one by Herman Finer are reprinted in *Bureaucratic Power in National Politics*, edited by F. E. Rourke, 1965.

10 As does W. W. Boyer, *Bureaucracy on Trial: Policy Making by Government Agencies*, 1964, p. 169.

11 A useful analysis of the Friedrich-Finer dispute is R. F. Bunn's "Notes on the Control and Responsibility of the Bureaucrat", *South Western Social Science Quarterly*, Vol. 41, 1961.

12 For an example of emphasis being placed on professionalism in civil services see P. Monypenny, "Professional Organizations and Bureaucratic Government", *South Western Social Science Quarterly*, Vol. 32, 1952. For stress on public contact see F. Morstein Marx, "Bureaucracy and Consultation", *Review of Politics*, Vol. 1, 1939.

13 J. D. Kingsley, op. cit., p. 269.

14 See Lord Attlee, "Civil Servants, Ministers, Parliament and the Public", in W. A. Robson, ed., *The Civil Service in Britain and France*, 1956.

15 G. Sjöberg, R. A. Brymer and B. Farris, "Bureaucracy and the Lower Class", *Sociology and Social Research*, Vol. 50, 1966.

16 For a general account of the activities of administrators designed to influence the political process see P. Woll, *American Bureaucracy*, 1963. For a journalist's account of a British case see S. Brittan, *The Treasury under the Tories, 1951–64*, 1964. However, it should be noted that C. Wright Mills does not regard the American professional administrator as part of the power élite, and believes that party patronage has prevented the rise of an independent federal administration. See *The Power Elite*, 1956, Galaxy edn, 1959, pp. 237–41.

17 F. E. Rourke, "Secrecy in American Bureaucracy", *Political Science Quarterly*, Vol. 72, 1957; "Bureaucracy and Public Opinion" in *Bureaucratic Power in National Politics*, edited by F. E. Rourke, 1965.

18 See C. K. Allen, *Bureaucracy Triumphant*, 1931; A. Diamant, "French Council of State", *Journal of Politics*, Vol. 13, 1951.

19 Both Harold Laski, *Parliamentary Government in England*, 1938, p. 151, and Sir Ivor Jennings, *The British Constitution*, 1941, pp. 131–4 regard the parliamentary question as effective in securing control throughout the civil service hierarchy. For a defence of congressional control of the American federal service see C. E. Gilbert and M. M. Kampelman, "Legislative Control of the Bureaucracy", *Annals of the American Academy of Political and Social Science*, Vol. 292, 1954.

20 W. W. Boyer, op. cit., chapter 7, "Assuring Public Responsibility".

21 Herman Finer, in F. E. Rourke, op. cit., p. 176.

22 *Public Administration and the Public Interest*, 1936, p. 22.

23 "Staff and Management Controls", *Annals of the American Academy of Political and Social Science*, Vol. 292, 1954.

24 R. Bendix, *Higher Civil Servants in American Society*, 1949, sets out to show that there can be no such thing as neutral executors of legislative enactments.

25 C. J Friedrich and T. Cole, op. cit., p. 88.

26 C. J. Friedrich, "Public Policy and the Nature of Administrative Responsibility", op. cit.

27 See N. E. Long, "Bureaucracy and Constitutionalism", *American Political Science Review*, Vol. 46, 1952, and "Public Policy and Administration: the Goals of Rationality and Responsibility", *Public Administration Review*, Vol. 14, 1954.

28 *Decentralization of Authority in a Bureaucracy*, 1961, p. 161.

29 For an examination of the possibility of professional isolation from the community see L. Urwick, "Bureaucracy and Democracy", *Public Administration*, Vol. 14, 1936.

30 For instance by N. E. Long, op. cit., and by C. E. Jacob in *Policy and Bureaucracy*, 1966.

31 *The Federal Government Service*, edited by W. S. Sayre, 1965, pp. 1–6.

32 P. Woll, op. cit., p. 174.

33 "Public Policy and the Nature of Administrative Responsibility", in F. E. Rourke, op. cit., p. 175.

34 p. 380.

35 See above, Ch. 4, pp. 68–71.

36 *Principles of Political Economy*, Vol. 2, chapter XI, "Limits of the Province of Government", p. 528.

37 G. Sjöberg, et al., op. cit., mention several examples of attempts to devise non-bureaucratic systems of organization. B. Coughlin, "Private Welfare in a Public Welfare Bureaucracy', *Social Service Review*, Vol. 35, 1961, examines how private associations may retain their independence from public welfare agencies.

Conclusion: The Concept of Bureaucracy in Social and Political Science

1 One of the best is still E. Barker's *The Development of Public Services in Western Europe 1660–1930*, 1944.

2 See A. Sauvy, *La Bureaucratie*, 1956, pp. 23 ff.

3 See R. Bendix, *Work and Authority in Industry*, 1956, pp. 198–253.

4 R. von Mohl, op. cit., p. 103.

5 In the work of R. H. Hall, F. Heady, C. R. Hinings et al.

Bibliography

Select

This list comprises only easily accessible books in English which can provide a useful introduction to the themes of the respective chapters of this volume.

General

MERTON, R. K. et al. (eds), *Reader in Bureaucracy*, The Free Press, Glencoe, Ill. 1952. Contains many of the most influential contributions to the literature about bureaucracy, including selections from Weber, Michels, Friedrich, Merton and Gouldner, and also a good general bibliography.

1/The Emergence of the Concept

MILL, J. S., *Considerations on Representative Government*, Parker, London 1861. The brief references to bureaucracy in this classic work summarize much of nineteenth-century theory on this subject.

2/The Classical Formulations

MOSCA, GAETANO, *The Ruling Class*, McGraw-Hill, New York 1939 (first Italian edition, 1896). The idea of bureaucracy becomes, for the first time, a key concept in a general theory of politics.

WEBER, MAX, "Bureaucracy", being Chapter VIII of *From Max Weber: Essays in Sociology*, edited by H. H. Gerth and C. Wright Mills, Oxford University Press, London and New York 1946. The most important source for modern theory.

3/The Debate with Weber

GOULDNER, ALVIN W., *Patterns of Industrial Bureaucracy*, The Free Press, Glencoe, Ill. 1954. A critical discussion of Weber in the light of a case study of an American factory.

BLAU, PETER M., *The Dynamics of Bureaucracy*, University of Chicago Press, Chicago 1955, rev. edn 1963. Similar in intent to Gouldner's study, but studies two public administration agencies.

4/Bureaucracy and the Ideologists

DJILAS, MILOVAN, *The New Class*, Thames and Hudson, London 1957. The culminating expression of Marxist dilemmas concerning bureaucracy.

NEUMANN, SIGMUND, *Permanent Revolution*, Pall Mall, London, 2nd edn 1965; Praeger, New York, 2nd edn 1965 (1st edn Harper, New York 1942). Contains a good, brief account of totalitarian reactions to the problem of bureaucracy.

VON MISES, LUDWIG, *Bureaucracy*, Yale University Press, New Haven 1944. An example of the conservative indictment of the state.

5/Seven Modern Concepts of Bureaucracy

CROZIER, MICHEL, *The Bureaucratic Phenomenon*, Tavistock, London 1964. Examines disabling features of two French organizations as examples of French culture patterns.

MARX, F. MORSTEIN, *The Administrative State*, Chicago University Press, Chicago 1957. A classification and analysis of public administration systems.

LA PALOMBARA, J. (ed.), *Bureaucracy and Political Development*, Princeton University Press, Princeton 1963. Includes papers by F. Morstein Marx, S. N. Eisenstadt, F. W. Riggs, M. Fainsod, W. R. Sharp and others.

6/Bureaucracy and the Theorists of Democracy

HYNEMAN. C. S., *Bureaucracy in a Democracy*, Harper, New York 1950. A broad and thorough consideration of the problems involved in the control of modern civil services.

ROURKE, F. E. (ed.), *Bureaucratic Power in National Politics*, Little, Brown & Co., Boston 1965. Includes important articles by Herman Finer and C. J. Friedrich on bureaucratic responsibility.

Works Cited

All works mentioned in the text are listed here with the exception of those already included in the Select Bibliography, above, and some early literary and lexicographical items for which full details have been given in the Notes and References. Books are cited according to the editions which were used for page references.

ALBROW, MARTIN, "The Study of Organizations—Objectivity or Bias?", in *Penguin Social Sciences Survey 1968*, edited by Julius Gould, Penguin Books, Harmondsworth, Middlesex 1968, pp. 146–67.

ALLEN, C. K., *Bureaucracy Triumphant*, Oxford University Press, London 1931.

ALMOND, G. A. and COLEMAN, J. S., *The Politics of Developing Areas*, Princeton University Press, Princeton 1960.

ANDERSON, T., *Masters of Russian Marxism*, Appleton Century Crofts, New York 1963.

Anonymous, "Der bureaukratische Staat nach seinem Ausgangspunkt und Ziel", *Deutsche Vierteljahreschrift*, Stuttgart 1857, pp. 107–47.

Anonymous, "The Encroaching Bureaucracy", *The Quarterly Review*, John Murray, London 1914, Vol. 221, pp. 51–75.

ARON, RAYMOND, *Main Currents in Sociological Thought*, Vol. 2, Weidenfeld and Nicolson, London 1968.

AVINERI, SHLOMO, *The Social and Political Thought of Karl Marx*, Cambridge University Press, London 1968.

AYLMER, G. E., *The King's Servants*, Routledge and Kegan Paul, London 1961.

BAGEHOT, WALTER, *The English Constitution*, Fontana, London 1963.

BAHRDT, H. P., *Industriebürokratie*, Ferdinand Enke, Stuttgart 1958.

BARKER, E., *The Development of Public Services in Western Europe 1660–1930*, Oxford University Press, London 1944.

BAUM, B. H., *The Decentralization of Authority in a Bureaucracy*, Prentice-Hall, Englewood Cliffs, N.J. 1961.

BAUMGARTEN, EDUARD, *Max Weber—Werk und Person*, J. C. B. Mohr, Tübingen 1964.

BECK, C., "Bureaucracy and Political Development in Eastern Europe", in *Bureaucracy and Political Development*, edited by J. La Palombara, 1963, pp. 268–300.

BECK, J. M., *Our Wonderland of Bureaucracy*, Macmillan, New York 1932.

BECKER, S. W. and GORDON, G., "An Entrepreneurial Theory of Formal Organizations. Part 1: Patterns of Formal Organization", *Administrative Science Quarterly*, Vol. 11, 1965–67, pp. 315–44.

BENDIX, R., "Bureaucracy: the problem and its setting", *American Sociological Review*, Vol. 12, 1947, pp. 493–507.

—— *Higher Civil Servants in American Society*, University of Colorado Studies, Boulder, Colorado 1949.

—— "Socialism and the theory of Bureaucracy", *Canadian Journal of Economics and Political Science*, Vol. 16, 1950, pp. 501–14.

—— *Work and Authority in Industry*, John Wiley, New York 1956.

—— *Max Weber—An Intellectual Portrait*, Heinemann, London 1960.

BENNIS, WARREN G., "The Coming Death of Bureaucracy", in *Behaviour in Organizations—a Multidimensional View*, edited by Anthony G. Athos and Robert E. Coffey, Prentice Hall, Englewood Cliffs, N.J. 1968, pp. 256–66.

BERGER, MORROE, *Bureaucracy and Society in Modern Egypt*, Princeton University Press, Princeton 1957.

BERNSTEIN, EDUARD, *Evolutionary Socialism*, I.L.P., London 1909.

BLACKIE, J. S., "Prussia and the Prussian System", *Westminster Review*, Vol. 37, 1842, pp. 135–71.

BLAU, P. M., *Bureaucracy in Modern Society*, Random House, New York 1956.

BLAU, P. M. and SCOTT, W. RICHARD, *Formal Organizations*, Routledge and Kegan Paul, London 1963.

BOYER, W. W., *Bureaucracy On Trial—Policy Making by Government Agencies*, Bobbs-Merrill, Indianapolis and New York 1964.

BRECHT, A., "How Bureaucracies Develop and Function", *Annals of the American Academy of Political and Social Science*, Vol. 292, 1954, pp. 1–10.

BRITTAN, SAMUEL, *The Treasury under the Tories 1951–64*, Penguin Books, Harmondsworth, Middlesex 1964.

BRUMBERG, A., "Soviet Campaign against Survivals of Capitalism", *Russian Review*, Vol. 12, 1953, pp. 65–78.

BUNN, R. F., "Notes on the control and responsibility of the bureaucrat", *South Western Social Science Quarterly*, Vol. 41, 1961, pp. 407–14.

BURIN, F. S., "Bureaucracy and National Socialism: A Reconsideration of Weberian Theory", in *Reader in Bureaucracy*, edited by R. K. Merton et al., 1952, pp. 33–47.

BURNHAM, JAMES, *The Managerial Revolution*, Penguin Books, Harmondsworth, Middlesex 1962.

CAMPBELL, G. A., *The Civil Service in Britain*, Penguin Books, Harmondsworth, Middlesex 1955.

CARLYLE, THOMAS, "The New Downing Street", *Latter Day Pamphlets: Collected Works*, Vol. 19, Chapman and Hall, London 1870.

CARTER, GWENDOLEN M. and BROWN, WILLIAM O., *Transition in Africa—Studies in Political Adaptation*, Boston University Press, Boston 1958.

CHEN PO-TA, *Mao Tse-tung on the Chinese Revolution*, Foreign Languages Press, Peking 1953.

COHEN, H., *The Demonics of Bureaucracy*, Iowa State University Press, Ames, Iowa 1965.

COLE, G. D. H., *History of Socialist Thought*, Macmillan, London 1963.

COLE, R. TAYLOR, "Italy's Fascist Bureaucracy", *American Political Sciences Review*, Vol. 32, 1938, pp. 1143–57.
———— *The Canadian Bureaucracy*, Duke University Press, Durham, N.C. 1949.
CONSTAS, HELEN, "Max Weber's Two Conceptions of Bureaucracy", *American Journal of Sociology*, Vol. 63, 1957–58, pp. 400–9.
CORPUZ, ONOFRE D., *The Bureaucracy in the Philippines*, Institute of Public Administration, University of the Philippines, Manila 1957.
———— "Theoretical Limitations of Max Weber's Systematic Analysis of Bureaucracy", *Philippine Journal of Public Administration*, Vol. 1, 1957, pp. 342–9.
COUGHLIN, B., "Private Welfare in a Public Welfare Bureaucracy", *Social Service Review*, Vol. 35, 1961, pp. 184–93.
CREEL, H. G., "The Beginnings of Bureaucracy in China: The Origin of the Hsien", *Journal of Asian Studies*, Vol. 23, 1964, pp. 155–84.
CRIDER, J. H., *The Bureaucrat*, J. B. Lippincott, Philadelphia and New York 1944.
CROSLAND, C. A. R., *The Future of Socialism*, Jonathan Cape, London 1956.
CROSSMAN, R. H. S., *Planning for Freedom*, Hamish Hamilton, London 1965.
DAHL, R. A. and LINDBLOM, C. E., *Politics, Economics and Welfare*, Harper, New York 1953.
DANIELS, R. V., *The Conscience of the Revolution—Communist Opposition in Soviet Russia*, Harvard University Press, Cambridge, Mass. 1960.
DELANEY, W., "The Development and Decline of Patrimonial and Bureaucratic Administrations", *Administrative Science Quarterly*, Vol. 7, 1962–63, pp. 458–501.
DIAMANT, A., "French Council of State: comparative observations on the problem of controlling the bureaucracy of the modern state", *Journal of Politics*, Vol. 13, 1951, pp. 562–88.
DIMOCK, MARSHALL E., "Bureaucracy Self-Examined", *Public Administration Review*, Vol. 4, 1944, pp. 197–207.
———— *Administrative Vitality*, Routledge and Kegan Paul, London 1960.
DJORDEVIC, J., "Local Self-Government in Yugoslavia", *American Slavic and East European Review*, Vol. 12, 1953, pp. 188–200.
DORSEY, J. T., "The Bureaucracy and Political Development in Vietnam", in *Bureaucracy and Political Development*, edited by J. La Palombara, 1963, pp. 318–59.
DOWNS, A., "Theory of Bureaucracy", *American Economic Review*, Vol. 55, 1965, pp. 439–46.
DRAPER, THEODORE, *Castroism: Theory and Practice*, Pall Mall Press, London 1965.
DUMONT, R., *Cuba, Socialisme et Développement*, Editions du Seuil, Paris 1964.
———— *Lands Alive*, The Merlin Press, London 1965.
EASTON, DAVID, *A Systems Analysis of Political Life*, John Wiley, New York 1965.
EISENSTADT, S. N., "Bureaucracy and Bureaucratization", *Current Sociology*, Vol. 7, 1958, pp. 97–164.
———— *The Political Systems of Empires*, The Free Press, Glencoe, Ill. 1963.
EMGE, CARL A., "Bürokratisierung unter philosophischer und soziologischer Sicht", *Kölner Zeitschrift für Soziologie*, Vol. 3, 1950–51, pp. 179–95.
ETZIONI, AMITAI, *Modern Organizations*, Prentice-Hall, Englewood Cliffs, N.J. 1964.
FAINSOD, M., "Bureaucracy and Modernization: The Russian and Soviet Case", in *Bureaucracy and Political Development*, edited by J. La Palombara, 1963, pp. 233–267.

FINER, HERMAN, "Le 'Service Civil' en Angleterre", *Revue des Sciences Politiques*, Vol. 50, 1927, pp. 11–40, 219–41.

——— "Critics of 'Bureaucracy' ", *Political Science Quarterly*, Vol. 60, 1945, pp. 100–12.

——— "Administrative Responsibility in Democratic Government", in *Bureaucratic Power in National Politics*, edited by F. E. Rourke, 1965, pp. 176–87.

FISCHEL, EDUARD, *Die Verfassung Englands*, Schneider, Berlin 1862.

FRANCIS, R. G. and STONE, R. C., *Service and Procedure in Bureaucracy*, University of Minnesota Press, Minneapolis 1956.

FRIEDMAN, GEORGES, *Industrial Society*, The Free Press, Glencoe, Ill. 1955.

FRIEDRICH, CARL J., "Public Policy and the Nature of Administrative Responsibility", in *Bureaucratic Power in National Politics*, edited by F. E. Rourke, 1965, pp. 165–75.

——— "Some Observations on Weber's Analysis of Bureaucracy", in *Reader in Bureaucracy*, edited by R. K. Merton et al., 1952, pp. 27–33.

FRIEDRICH, CARL J. and COLE, R. TAYLOR, *Responsible Bureaucracy: A Study of the Swiss Civil Service*, Harvard University Press, Cambridge, Mass. 1932.

GABLENTZ, O. H., "Industriebürokratie", *Schmollers Jahrbuch*, Vol. 50, 1926, pp. 539–72.

GEHLEN, A., "Bürokratisierung", *Kölner Zeitschrift für Soziologie*, Vol. 3, 1950–51, pp. 195–208.

GILBERT, C. E. and KAMPELMAN, M. M., "Legislative Control of the Bureaucracy", *Annals of the American Academy of Political and Social Science*, Vol. 292, 1954, pp. 76–87.

GÖRRES, J. J., *Deutschland und die Revolution*, Metzler, Stuttgart 1821.

——— *Europa und die Revolution*, Metzler, Stuttgart 1819.

GOULD, JULIUS and KOLB, W. L. (eds), *A Dictionary of the Social Sciences*, Tavistock Publications, London 1964.

GOULDNER, A., "Metaphysical Pathos and the Theory of Bureaucracy", *American Political Science Review*, Vol. 49, 1955, pp. 496–507.

GREEN, A. S., "Growing Bureaucracy and Parliamentary Decline", *Nineteenth Century*, Vol. 47, 1900, pp. 839–46.

GRIMOND, J., "Bureaucrats in the Saddle", *The Guardian*, Manchester, Jan. 8, 1968.

HALL, R. H., "Concept of Bureaucracy—an Empirical Assessment", *American Journal of Sociology*, Vol. 69, 1963, pp. 32–40.

HANDMAN, MAX, "The Bureaucratic Culture Pattern and Political Revolutions", *American Journal of Sociology*, Vol. 39, 1933, pp. 301–13.

HEADY, FERREL, *Public Administration: a Comparative Perspective*, Prentice-Hall, Englewood Cliffs, N.J. 1966.

HEGEL, G. W. F., *Hegel's Philosophy of Right*, translated by T. M. Knox, Oxford University Press, London 1942.

HEINZEN, K., *Die Preussische Büreaukratie*, Leske, Darmstadt 1845.

HERRING, E. PENDELTON, *Public Administration and the Public Interest*, McGraw-Hill, New York 1936.

HEWART, LORD, *The New Despotism*, Ernest Benn, London 1929.

HININGS, C. R., PUGH, D. S., HICKSON, D. J., TURNER, C., "An Approach to the Study of Bureaucracy", *Sociology*, Vol. 1, 1967, pp. 61–72.

HITLER, ADOLF, *My Struggle (Mein Kampf)*, Hurst and Blackett, London 1938.

HOSELITZ, B. F., "Levels of Economic Performance and Bureaucratic Structure", in *Bureaucracy and Political Development*, edited by J. La Palombara, 1963, pp. 168–98.

HUMBOLDT, W. VON, *Ideen zu einem Versuch die Gränzen der Wirksamkeit des Staats zu bestimmen*, Trewendt, Breslau 1851.

JACOB, C. E., *Policy and Bureaucracy*, van Nostrand, New York 1966.

JACOBS, P. and LANDAU, S. (eds), *The New Radicals*, Penguin Books, Harmondsworth, Middlesex 1966.

JARVIE, I. C. and AGASSI, JOSEPH, "The problem of the rationality of magic", *British Journal of Sociology*, Vol. 18, 1967, pp. 55–74.

JENNINGS, W. I., *The British Constitution*, Cambridge University Press, London 1941.

JOHNSON, H. C., "Concept of Bureaucracy in Cameralism", *Political Science Quarterly*, Vol. 79, 1964, pp. 378–402.

KAUTSKY, KARL, *The Labour Revolution*, Allen and Unwin, London 1925.

KEETON, G. W., *The Passing of Parliament*, Ernest Benn, London 1952.

KINGSLEY, J. D., *Representative Bureaucracy*, Antioch Press, Yellow Springs, Ohio 1944.

LANDAUER, E., "Kapitalistischer Geist und Verwaltungsbürokratie in Öffentlichen Unternehmungen", *Schmollers Jahrbuch*, Vol. 54, 1930, pp. 505–21.

LAPENNA, I., *State and Law: Soviet and Yugoslav Theory*, The Athlone Press, London 1964.

LASKI, HAROLD, "Bureaucracy", *Encyclopaedia of the Social Sciences*, Vol. 3, Macmillan, New York 1930, pp. 70–4.

—— *Parliamentary Government in England*, Allen and Unwin, London 1938.

LASSWELL, H. D. and KAPLAN, ABRAHAM, *Power and Society: A Framework for Political Enquiry*, Yale University Press, New Haven 1950.

LE PLAY, F., *La Réforme Sociale en France*, Plon, Paris 1864.

LENIN, V. I., "The State and the Revolution", in *Collected Works*, Vol. 25, Foreign Languages Publishing House, Moscow 1964.

LEONARD, PETER, *Sociology in Social Work*, Routledge and Kegan Paul, London 1966.

LEROY-BEAULIEU, P., *L'État Moderne et ses Fonctions*, Guillaumin, Paris 1890.

LICHTHEIM, G., *Marxism*, Routledge and Kegan Paul, London 1961.

—— *Marxism in Modern France*, Columbia University Press, New York 1966.

LITWAK, E. and MEYER, H. J., "A Balance Theory of Co-ordination between Bureaucratic Organizations and Community Primary Groups", *Administrative Science Quarterly*, Vol. 11, 1966–67, pp. 31–58.

LONG, N. E., "Bureaucracy and Constitutionalism", *American Political Science Review*, Vol. 46, 1952, pp. 808–18.

—— "Public Policy and Administration: The Goals of Rationality and Responsibility", *Public Administration Review*, Vol. 14, 1954, pp. 22–31.

LUXEMBURG, ROSA, *The Russian Revolution and Leninism or Marxism*, edited by B. D. Wolfe, University of Michigan, Ann Arbor 1961.

MALCHUS, C. A. VON, *Politik der inneren Staatsverwaltung*, Mohr, Heidelberg 1823.

MANGOLD, K. P., "Lenin's Cardinal Rules of Poverty and Recall: Neglected Ideological Weapons for the West", *Orbis*, Vol. 8, 1964–65, pp. 955–71.

MANNHEIM, KARL, *Freedom, Power and Democratic Planning*, Routledge and Kegan Paul, London 1951.

MAO TSE-TUNG, *The Thoughts of Chairman Mao Tse-tung*, Anthony Gibbs, London 1967.

MARCH, J. G. and SIMON, HERBERT A., *Organizations*, John Wiley, New York 1958.

MARX, F. MORSTEIN, "German Bureaucracy in Transition", *American Political Science Review*, Vol. 28, 1934, pp. 467–80.

——— "Bureaucracy and Consultation", *Review of Politics*, Vol. 1, 1939, pp. 84–100.

——— "Bureaucracy and Dictatorship", *Review of Politics*, Vol. 3, 1941, pp. 100–17.

MARX, KARL and ENGELS, FRIEDRICH, *Marx-Engels Gesamtausgabe*, Marx-Engels Institute, Moscow 1927 onwards.

——— *Basic Writings on Politics and Philosophy*, edited by L. S. Feuer, Doubleday, New York 1959.

——— *The German Ideology*, Foreign Languages Publishing House, Moscow 1965.

MAXIMOFF, G. P. (ed.), *The Political Philosophy of Bakunin: Scientific Anarchism*, The Free Press, Glencoe, Ill. 1953.

MAYNTZ, R., "Max Weber's Ideal typus der Bürokratie und die Organisations-Soziologie", *Kölner Zeitschrift für Soziologie und Sozialpsychologie*, Vol. 17, 1965, pp. 493–502.

MEISEL, J. H., *The Myth of the Ruling Class*, University of Michigan, Ann Arbor 1958.

MERTON, R. K., "Bureaucratic Structure and Personality", in *Reader in Bureaucracy*, edited by R. K. Merton et al., The Free Press, Glencoe, Ill. 1952, pp. 361–71.

MEYER, A. G., *Leninism*, Harvard University Press, Cambridge, Mass. 1957.

MEYNAUD, JEAN, *Technocracy*, Faber and Faber, London 1968.

MICHELS, ROBERT, *Political Parties*, Collier Books, New York 1962.

MILL, J. S., *On Liberty*, Longmans Green, London 1892.

——— *Principles of Political Economy*, Parker, London 1848.

MILLS, C. WRIGHT, *The Power Elite*, Galaxy Books, New York 1959.

MOHL, ROBERT VON, *Staatsrecht, Völkerrecht und Politik*, Laupp, Tübingen 1862.

MONTAGUE, F. C., *The Limits of Individual Liberty*, Rivingtons, London 1885.

MONYPENNY, P., "Professional Organizations and Bureaucratic Government", *South Western Social Science Quarterly*, Vol. 32, 1952, pp. 257–63.

MOSCA, GAETANO, *Sulla Teorica dei Governi e sul Governo Parlamentare*, Loescher, Rome 1884.

MOUZELIS, N. P., *Organization and Bureaucracy: An Analysis of Modern Theories*, Routledge and Kegan Paul, London 1967.

MUIR, RAMSAY, *Peers and Bureaucrats*, Constable, London 1910.

MUSSOLINI, BENITO, *The Corporate State*, Vallachi, Florence 1938.

——— *The Doctrine of Fascism*, Ardita, Rome 1935.

——— *My Autobiography*, Hutchinson, London n.d.

NAVILLE, P., *Le Nouveau Leviathan 1: De l'Alienation à la Jouissance*, Riviere, Paris 1957.

NETTL, J. P., *Political Mobilization*, Faber and Faber, London 1967.

NEUMANN, FRANZ, *Behemoth. The Structure and Practice of National Socialism*, Gollancz, London 1942.

OBERSCHALL, A., *Empirical Social Research in Germany, 1848–1914*, Mouton, The Hague 1965.

O'DONNEL, ARNOUT, "State Education in France", *Blackwood's Edinburgh Magazine*, Vol. 40, 1836, pp. 579–94.

OLSZEWSKI, J., *Bureaukratie*, Stuber, Würzburg 1904.

PARSONS, TALCOTT, *Structure and Process in Modern Societies*, The Free Press, Glencoe, Ill. 1960.

PIPES, RICHARD, "Max Weber et la Russie", *Le Contrat Social*, Vol. 4, Paris 1960, pp. 71–6.

PRESTHUS, R. V., "Weberian v. Welfare Bureaucracy in Traditional Society", *Administrative Science Quarterly*, Vol. 6, 1961–62, pp. 1–24.

———— *The Organizational Society*, Knopf, New York 1962.

RENNER, KARL, *Demokratie und Bureaukratie*, Europa Verlag, Vienna 1947.

RIGGS, F. W., "Agraria and Industria: Toward a Typology of Public Administration", in *Toward the Comparative Study of Public Administration*, edited by W. J. Siffin, 1957, pp. 23–116.

———— *Administration in Developing Countries: The Theory of Prismatic Society*, Houghton Mifflin, Boston 1964.

———— "Bureaucracy and Political Development: A Paradoxical View", in *Bureaucracy and Poltical Development*, edited by J. La Palombara, 1963, pp. 120–67.

RIZZI, B. ("Bruno R."), *La Bureaucratisation du Monde*, Hachette, Paris 1939.

ROBSON, W. A. (ed.), *The Civil Service in Britain and France*, The Hogarth Press, London 1956.

ROHMER, FRIEDRICH, *Deutschlands alte und neue Bureaukratie*, Kaiser, Munich 1848.

ROSENBERG, ALFRED, *Der Mythus des 20 Jahrhunderts*, Hoheneichen Verlag, Munich 1943.

———— *Blut und Ehre*, N.S.D.A.P., Munich 1936.

ROURKE, F. E., "Secrecy in American Bureaucracy", *Political Science Quarterly*, Vol. 72, 1957, pp. 540–64.

———— "Bureaucracy and Public Opinion", in *Bureaucratic Power in National Politics*, edited by F. E. Rourke, Little, Brown & Co., Boston 1965, pp. 188–99.

SANTANGELO SPOTO, I., "La Burocrazia e il Governo Parlamentare", in *Biblioteca di Scienze Politiche e Amministrative*, edited by A. Brunialti, Turin 1902, pp. 1–511.

SAUVAGEOT, J. et al., *The Student Revolt*, Panther Books, London 1968.

SAUVY, A., *La Bureaucratie*, P.U.F., Paris 1956.

SAYRE, WALLACE S., "Bureaucracies: Some Contrasts in Systems", *Indian Journal of Public Administration*, Vol. 10, 1964, pp. 219–29.

SAYRE, WALLACE S. (ed.), *The Federal Government Service*, Prentice-Hall, Englewood Cliffs, N.J. 1965.

SCHACHTMAN, M., *The Bureaucratic Revolution*, Donald Press, New York 1962.

SCHMITT, CARL, *Verfassungsrechtliche Aufsatze 1924–54*, Duncker und Humblot, Berlin 1958.

SCHMIDT, CARL T., *The Corporate State in Action: Italy under Fascism*, Oxford University Press, New York 1939.

SCHMOLLER, G., "Die Behördenorganisation und die allgemeine Staatsverwaltung Preussens im 18 Jahrhundert", in *Acta Borussica*, edited by G. Schmoller, Vol. 1, Parey, Berlin 1894, pp. 1–141.

———— "Der deutsche Beamtenstaat vom 16 bis 18 Jahrundert", *Umrisse und Untersuchungen zur Verfassungs-, Verwaltungs- und Wirtschaftsgeschichte*, Duncker und Humblot, Berlin 1898, pp. 289–313.

SCHULTE, F. VON, "Bureaucracy and its Operation in Germany and Austria-Hungary", *Contemporary Review*, Vol. 37, 1880, pp. 432–58.

SCHUMPETER, J. A., *Capitalism, Socialism and Democracy*, Allen and Unwin, London 1950.

SELZNICK, P., "An Approach to a Theory of Bureaucracy", *American Sociological Review*, Vol. 8, 1943, pp. 47–54.

———— *TVA and the Grass Roots*, Harper Torchbooks, New York 1966.

SERENO, R., "The Anti-Aristotelianism of Gaetano Mosca and its Fate", *Ethics*, Vol. 48, 1937–38, pp. 509–18.

SHARP, W. R., "Le Développement de la Bureaucratie aux États-Unis", *Revue des Sciences Politiques*, Vol. 50, 1927, pp. 393–415, 539–54.

SIFFIN, W. J. (ed.), *Toward the Comparative Study of Public Administration*, Indiana University Press, Bloomington, Indiana 1957.

SILBERMAN, B. S., "Bureaucracy and Economic Development in Japan", *Asian Survey*, Vol. 5, 1965, pp. 529–37.

SIMON, HERBERT A., *Administrative Behavior*, Macmillan, New York 1957.

—— "Staff and Management Controls", *Annals of the American Academy of Political and Social Science*, Vol. 292, 1954, pp. 95–103.

SJÖBERG, G., BRYMER, R. A. and FARRIS, B., "Bureaucracy and the Lower Class", *Sociology and Social Research*, Vol. 50, 1966, pp. 325–37.

SMEND, Rudolf, *Staatsrechtliche Abhandlungen und andere Aufsatze*, Duncker und Humblot, Berlin 1955.

SPENCER, HERBERT, "Specialized Administration", in *Essays Scientific, Political and Speculative* by Herbert Spencer, Williams and Norgate, London 1891, pp. 401–44.

—— *The Man versus the State*, Williams and Norgate, London 1885.

—— *The Study of Sociology*, Ann Arbor Paperbacks, 1961.

SPITZER, A. B., "Bureaucrat as Pro-consul: The Restoration Prefect and the Police Générale", *Comparative Studies in Society and History*, Vol. 7, 1965, pp. 371–92.

STALIN, J., *Leninism*, Allen and Unwin, London 1928.

STAMMER, OTTO, "Bürokratie", in *Handbuch der Soziologie*, edited by W. Ziegenfuss, F. Enke, Stuttgart 1956, pp. 601–3.

STAWAR, ANDRÉ, *Libres Essais Marxistes*, Editions du Seuil, Paris 1963.

STEIN, LORENZ VON, *Die Verwaltungslehre*, Cotta, Stuttgart 1869.

STEWART, R., *The Reality of Management*, Heinemann, London 1963.

STINCHCOMBE, A. L., "Bureaucratic and Craft Administration of Production: A Comparative Study", *Administrative Science Quarterly*, Vol. 4, 1959–60, pp. 168–87.

STRAUSS, E., *The Ruling Servants*, Allen and Unwin, London 1961.

STROUP, H., *Bureaucracy in Higher Education*, Free Press, New York 1966.

SULLIVAN, L., *Bureaucracy Runs Amuck*, Bobbs-Merrill, Indianapolis and New York 1944.

—— *The Dead Hand of Bureaucracy*, Bobbs-Merrill, Indianapolis and New York 1940.

SULTAN, H. and ABENDROTH, W., *Bürokratische Verwaltungsstaat und Soziale Demokratie*, O. Goedel, Hannover and Frankfurt a.M. 1955.

TOCQUEVILLE, A. DE, *L'Ancien Régime et la Révolution*, C. Lévy, Paris 1877.

TROTSKY, L., *The New Course*, University of Michigan, Ann Arbor 1965.

—— *The Revolution Betrayed*, Doubleday, New York 1937.

TULLOCK, G., *The Politics of Bureaucracy*, Public Affairs Press, Washington, D.C. 1965.

UDY, S. R., "Bureaucracy and Rationality in Weber's Organization Theory", *American Sociological Review*, Vol. 24, 1959, pp. 791–5.

URWICK, L., "Bureaucracy and Democracy", *Public Administration*, Vol. 14, 1936, pp. 134–49.

VIVIEN, L., *Études Administratives*, Guillaumin, Paris 1845.

WARNOTTE, D., "Bureaucratie et Fonctionnairisme", *Revue de l'Institut de Sociologie, Université Libre de Bruxelles*, Vol. 17, 1937, pp. 218–60.

WEBER, ALFRED, "Der Beamte", in *Ideen zur Staats- und Kultursoziologie*, G. Braun, Karlsruhe 1927, pp. 81–101.

WEBER, MAX, *Gesammelte Politische Schriften*, J. C. B. Mohr, Tübingen 1958.
——— *Max Weber on Law in Economy and Society*, edited by Max Rheinstein, Harvard University Press, Cambridge, Mass. 1954.
——— *The Methodology of the Social Sciences*, translated and edited by E. A. Shils and H. A. Finch, The Free Press, Glencoe, Ill. 1949.
——— *The Theory of Social and Economic Organization*, translated by A. M. Henderson and Talcott Parsons, The Free Press, Glencoe, Ill. 1947.
——— *Wirtschaft und Gesellschaft*, J. C. B. Mohr, Tübingen 1956.
WILLIAMS, RAYMOND (ed.), *May Day Manifesto 1968*, Penguin Books, Harmondsworth, Middlesex 1968.
WITTFOGEL, KARL A., *Oriental Despotism*, Yale University Press, New Haven 1957.
——— "Ruling Bureaucracy of Oriental Despotism: A Phenomenon that Paralyzed Marx", *Review of Politics*, Vol. 15, 1953, pp. 350–9.
WOLL, P., *American Bureaucracy*, W. W. Norton, New York 1963.
YANG, C. K., "Some Characteristics of Chinese Bureaucratic Behaviour", in *Confucianism in Action*, edited by D. S. Nivison and A. F. Wright, Stanford University Press, Stanford, California 1959, pp. 134–64.

Index